SMART Social Media For Authors:
The practical guide for anyone to sell more books

by **Chris Syme**

Why Authors Need This Book

If you bought this book because you are confused about how to use social media to sell your books, you are in the right place. You may already be using social media to build a fan base around your books, but you'd like to learn how to use it more effectively. This book is for you. If you are a skeptic, I think you'll like my premise that one size doesn't fit all when it comes to marketing.

Book marketing works best if you are open to learning. Today's authors, especially indie authors, need to learn the art of book promotion in order to stay competitive. Part of your job as an author is getting your books in front of the right readers. And unless you are a top seller, Amazon isn't going to do that for you.

You need to have some sort of marketing strategy in order to be discovered in this noisy, saturated market of books. And I guarantee that you will come away from this book with a simple plan that will work for you—because you put it together.

Whether we like it or not, authors are marketers. Your livelihood depends on it. Even if you get a book contract, you should implement SMART social media strategies to help boost your sales and build an army of loyal fans.

Many marketers are doing authors a disservice. Much of the social media marketing advice I see aimed at authors is either tool-centric or borderline unethical. It's time for an approach to social media marketing for authors that is both strategic and uncomplicated—one that teaches authors to take charge of marketing not just their books, but their whole author brand. That's why I developed the SMART system.

What you won't get from this book is the panic-inducing message that every author needs to be on every social media platform out there. You will get this message: every author needs a plan to market their books and connect with their fans, and SMART social media should be a part of that plan.

My focus is on the approach, not specialized apps or social media platforms, which are tools. Talking only about tools is a recipe for disaster. Tools change daily. As I write this in the summer of 2015, Facebook has made two major changes to their brand page algorithm in one month. If I write a book about tools, it will be obsolete before it hits publication. Tool-centric social media advice only works in the context of a plan. Without the plan, it is like throwing darts blindfolded. You may hit the target by accident, but your chances of hitting the bull's-eye will go way up if you take the blindfold off and see what you're aiming at.

A Word About Amazon

There is much written today about how social media is a waste of time and does not sell books. Naysayers have case studies and data to prove this theory, but beware. The truth is that you don't need to have 20,000 followers on Facebook to sell books there. This book takes for granted that authors need to understand how to use Amazon as a marketing platform and have a baseline idea of how Amazon promotes and recommends books. Covers, book descriptions, the Look Inside page, and keywords must be mastered in ordered to be successful on Amazon. But this book is not about marketing on Amazon.

How To Get The Most From This Book

This book will guide you through the process of learning how to sell books using social media effectively. But on that journey you will also learn that social media is about much more than sales. It will help you understand the concept of SMART social media and why your marketing efforts must be Sustainable, Manageable, Author-Specific, Relevant, and Tactics Last, Strategy First.

After we take a dive into each of those SMART components and find out how they are necessary for success, we will move on to some fundamentals. It's not enough to just understand why SMART social media is the best method for marketing your books. There are five fundamental skills that will help you be more successful as a marketer. They boost your marketing skill level in all areas, not just in social media. We cover each of those skills in Chapters 1 through 6.

When I was a high school basketball coach, I spent the majority of the practice time working on fundamentals—skill drills that involved dribbling, shooting, screening, passing, and more. Every part of game play relies on proficient execution of the fundamentals. Now before I lose you all in the sports metaphor, I'll cut to the takeaway. **You can't play the game to your full potential without knowing the fundamentals first.** Make a commitment to go through the action steps in Chapters 7 through 11 to cement the fundamentals in your thinking. You may not implement them exactly as I suggest, but they will help you figure out how they can best work for you with the time, resources, and skill set you have. Practice the fundamentals and you'll be a better player.

After we address the fundamentals, it's time to open the toolbox in Chapter 12 through 15. It's important to keep in mind that my working definition of social media may be much broader than yours. As a marketer, I think of social media as any media that is interactive and can foster two-way communication using digital channels. Yes, I do include websites and email newsletters in the toolbox. My reason is that both of these are intricately connected to social media. Successful websites and email campaigns need to loop to your branded social media channels. We need every tool in the box to build the house. I don't have a separate tool box for my website or my newsletter. They all live happily together.

You may be surprised that I do not have a laundry list of must-have social media channels here. I like to start with what I believe is absolutely necessary and then work from there. Every author is different. You all have different skillsets. Some of you have been at this social media thing for a while and some are just starting. For some of you, social media is like pulling teeth, for others it is an addiction. Some of you have a life—by that I mean some have another job, a family, partner, small children, or older parents to care for. SMART social media starts you right where you are today and helps you plot a map for your own journey of success.

In Chapter 15 we visit the Playground. I give you plenty of suggestions on how to add more tools, if you have the time. But here's the thing: you are a writer first. If you ever get to the place where you would rather be on Facebook all day, then you are falling into the trap of procrastination. Social media can be a distraction—kind of like binge watching on Netflix. So be careful on the playground.

In Chapters 16 and 17, you will learn the difference between long-term and short-term campaigns and why you need both. We'll talk about how SMART social media can help a book launch (short-term campaign) and how it can help you sell your backlist (long-term).

Chapter 18 focuses on social media advertising. We'll take a deeper dive into social media ads. I'll let you know what I think is working, what is not, and what platforms are not worth your dough... yet. We'll talk about why this component requires a methodical line item budget to work. Chapter 19 helps you stay away from unethical advertisers.

I wouldn't feel I did a good job if I didn't leave you with a list of resources in Chapter 20—both people and places—that will help you continue the journey to be a SMART social media marketer. I am not the only one out there with this message. There are several people in the publishing sector, in addition to really smart people in the business sector, who know way more about this stuff than I do. And I want to direct you to them.

At the end of every chapter you will find action points. I encourage you to put these on your calendar or to-do list. They will help you get the most out of the book.

At the end of the book there is a section called "Bonus Content" that leaves you with some free resources to help you continue your journey as a marketer. The section includes a signup for a free three-part video series on how to use Facebook for successful book marketing and a sample book launch template.

Why I Wrote This Book

I've been involved in writing, media relations, and marketing in one form or another professionally for over twenty years. I love marketing. I understand the power of good marketing and I know how to harness that power. My husband thinks I am crazy because I am more interested in TV commercials than the actual shows. But I know that not everybody feels the same as I do. That's why I wrote this book.

I have owned my own media agency for almost six years when I decided to leave my media relations job to care for my mother who was suffering from dementia. I was on the ground floor when social media came on the scene and have had the privilege of building award-winning social media campaigns. In 2014, my agency won the Social Media Agency Of The Year award from the SoMe Awards based in Portland, Oregon. This is my third book on social media.

So how did I get here? Two years ago my indie author daughter asked me to take on some of her marketing, so I started doing research on what was available in her sector. I was shocked at the lack of resources, especially ones that seemed to grasp the basic principles of strategic marketing. I was hooked on helping.

My mission since has been to bring SMART and simple strategic social media marketing to indie authors. I believe in the power of social media to boost sales, develop invested and loyal fan bases, and build brands quicker than traditional marketing alone ever could. But I also believe there are no shortcuts.

Indie authors can be successful marketing their own books. I am here to help.

Table Of Contents

Part I - The SMART Social Media Marketing Manifesto
Chapter 1: What Is SMART Social Media?
Chapter 2: SMART Social Media Is Sustainable
Chapter 3: SMART Social Media Is Manageable
Chapter 4: SMART Social Media Is Audience-Specific
Chapter 5: SMART Social Media Is Relevant
Chapter 6: SMART Social Media Means Tactics Last, Strategy First
Part II - SMART Fundamentals
Chapter 7: The Plan - Start With GOST
Chapter 8: Know Thy Audience
Chapter 9: Help Or Hype? To Sell Or Not To Sell
Chapter 10: The Marketing Mix
Chapter 11: Brand Advocates - How To Build Raving Fans
Part III - The SMART Social Media Marketing Toolbox
Chapter 12: Too Many Tools To Choose From
Chapter 13: The Big Three - Websites, Mailing Lists, And Facebook… Oh My
Chapter 14: The Next Three - Pinterest, Author Pages, And Blogs
Chapter 15: The Playground - How Much Social Media Is Enough?
Part IV - The SMART Campaign — It's All About Momentum
Chapter 16: What Is A Campaign?
Chapter 17: The Four Phases Of Short-Term Campaigns
Chapter 18: The SMART Way To Use Paid Online Ads To Boost Sales
Chapter 19: A Word Of Caution About Social Media Ads
Chapter 20: SMART Resources: People And Companies That You Can Trust
Copyright

About The Author

Chris Syme has over 20 years of experience in communications and marketing and is the owner of CKSyme Media Group, a consulting firm in Bozeman, Montana. Her agency specializes in digital marketing strategies, crisis communications, and marketing services for authors and publishers.

She is a frequent speaker at education and nonprofit conferences. She worked in media relations at Eastern Washington University where she did her graduate work in crisis management. She also worked at Montana State University where she directed social media efforts and event operations in the athletic department.

She is the author of three books: <u>Listen, Engage, Respond</u> (using social media as a crisis prevention and management tool) and <u>Practice Safe Social</u> (a model for responsible social media use training) and <u>Practice Safe Social 2.0</u>. In 2014, the CKSyme Media Group was honored as Social Media Agency Of The Year by the SoMe Social Media Awards in Portland, Oregon.

She and her husband Terry operate a grain farm and have two grown daughters.

Chris writes regularly about marketing and social media on her blog at cksyme.com and is featured on many national marketing sites including Social Media Today. You can connect with her on Twitter (@cksyme). She is also available for speaking engagements, guest blog posts, and podcast interviews. Please email chris@cksyme.com for more information.

Part I - The SMART Social Media Marketing Manifesto

The brief history of social media feels more like dog years than human years. Even though Friendster surfaced as the first social network in 2002, social media did not become a marketing channel until Facebook introduced "brand" pages in 2007, one year after Twitter arrived on the scene. In 2015, social media is no longer an afterthought in marketing circles. It is a necessary asset. And like every good historic movement, social media has a manifesto—a declaration of best practices which is continually evolving.

Chapter 1: What Is SMART Social Media?

SMART social media is made up of five components or necessary characteristics—each one beginning with a letter of the acronym SMART. The five are interconnected and are strongest when they stand together rather than alone. A winning marketing plan has all five: Sustainable, Manageable, Audience-Specific, Relevant, and Tactics Last.

How Social Media Has Changed the Way We Live

Social media has forever changed the way we live and do business. Its effect on marketing is seismic. It has changed the way we shop, eat, travel, work, date, raise our children, digest news, and communicate with friends and family. It is also volatile. It can take down a reputation in hours, bring a tragic news story halfway around the world to your phone in real time, and is a conduit for the darkest of human behaviors. It is rocket fuel. Its breakneck speed encourages shoddy reporting, turns gossip into fact, and creates impatient customers who think every tweet should be answered in 60 seconds by 140 characters or less. And it is also useful. It brings the world to our fingertips, keeps us in touch, and allows us glean a wealth of information with a few keystrokes.

When British computer scientist Sir Tim Berners-Lee created the first successful communication on what we know as the internet in 1989, he probably didn't envision quite where we would be today. From the first "web blog" created at Swarthmore College by student Justin Hall in 1991 to the recent release of a new video live streaming app called Periscope that turns any smartphone into a TV camera, we've come a long way, baby.

Pew Internet Research reported in September 2014 that 71 percent of online adults use social media and 52 percent use more than one platform. For the first time since Pew started reporting on social media, over half of online adults 65 and over are on Facebook. A whopping 84 percent of young adults ages 18 to 29 use Facebook.

The speed and critical mass of social media are a perfect storm for marketing. A significant 92 percent of marketers say social media is important to their marketing efforts, according to Social Media Examiner's 2015 Social Media Marketing Industry Report, which is an annual benchmark report for how marketers use social media.

Why Do I Need Social Media?

Authors must wear a marketing hat—no exceptions. Some don it grudgingly, others cannot seem to take it off and write. Some authors have such a large fan base from years of writing success that they don't need to market their books. But most of us need to market our products (yes, a book is a product—sorry). We are not all Stephen King or J.K. Rowling.

Authors need social media to help build a platform for visibility. Michael Hyatt defines a platform as "the thing you have to stand on to get heard". It's not a stage built of wood or metal. Today's platform is built with people—connections, contacts, followers. Whether you like it or not, you are building a platform. Your website, your email newsletter, your social media—they are all part of your platform because that is where people connect with you.

There are three types of platforms:

- **The drifting platform.** This platform has no real purpose and no real blueprint. Authors with a drifting platform are doing nothing to promote themselves or their books. Their books usually sell at an inconsistent rate. They just write, publish, and hope they sell enough books so Amazon will send their title out in an email recommending a sea of similar books. Books can take off with no promotion, especially if they are well-written or get promoted by influencers, but they are outliers. Don't bank on a drifting platform to make a living as an indie author.
- **The discoverability platform.** This platform helps an author's books get seen or discovered. Kristine Kathryn Rusch wrote an excellent book on discoverability and how to get your books seen by the right people. But discoverability is more about long-term visibility, not short-term sales.
- **The sales platform.** Building a sales platform is necessary for short-term sales. The sales platform is not a noisy, slippery series of get-rich-quick tactics that lead to selling millions of books. It blends both long-term discoverability and short-term sales methods together. It uses advertising methods designed to sell books quickly for a launch and slowly to promote your back list. This platform uses a number of different strategies of which social media is one.

As we go through the book you will see how social media is an important element to use for both discoverability and sales. It builds the deep connections and loyalty that promote long-term sales and creates the real-time excitement that propels prompt action.

SMART Social Media to the Rescue

Authors I talk with everywhere are craving an understandable social media marketing system that helps build a fan base and sell books. We see social media marketing advice that is all over the map. Unethical sites promise boatloads of retweets and book sales if you give them fifteen dollars. Marketers tell us to be on every social media channel, buy Facebook ads, don't buy Facebook ads, make your own book trailer, develop a community on Goodreads, and be sure and blog three times a week and tweet six times a day. It's enough to make you want to run to the window and shout, "I'm as mad as hell and I'm not going to take it anymore!"

Before you throw out the baby with the bathwater, I can promise you that SMART social media marketing does work, but it *takes* work. Your success will be proportional to your time, resources, skill level, and commitment—but you will have success. There is a learning curve, but anyone who can write a book can learn how to market that book. There are no shortcuts. You will have to do the time and make the effort. And copying others won't always work. Maybe they have more time, resources, and skill than you do. But implementing a successful system can make all the difference, no matter what your skill level is or how much time and resources you have at your disposal.

If you're feeling more than a little overwhelmed you might be thinking, *just because everybody is on social media doesn't mean it will work for me.* That is a good observation. Everybody doesn't need to use social media to market their books. But I can promise you that if you want to learn how to use it decisively, it will help you sell more books and build a loyal audience.

How about some data? I try not to make marketing decisions based on what I think. I like data-informed decisions because they yield the most predictable results. HubSpot, one of the top inbound marketing companies in the world, regularly researches consumer behavior related to social media. In this infographic (http://bit.ly/1Z0RQG3) on the growing trend of online sales, there is a statistic that is mind-boggling: 71 percent are more likely to make a purchase when referred by social media. And they are only seven percent likely to buy if not referred by social media.

Make no mistake. Social media is a springboard for sales. Facebook, Twitter, and Pinterest all have "buy now" features either active or coming online soon. Because of its convenience and its ability to turbo-boost word of mouth, social media is the new marketplace.

In the next five chapters we'll discuss each piece of the of SMART Social Media Marketing Manifesto in detail and how you can take and successfully apply each piece to your own marketing plan.

Action Steps

1. Start a journal and keep track of key observations and action steps from the book that will you want to revisit. Answer these two questions before you move on to Chapter 2:
-What role, if any, do you think social media should play in the promotion of your books and yourself as an author?
-Do any of those roles need developing now? Are there any social media is already fulfilling for you?
-What are the key issues you want answers to as you read this book?

Chapter 2: SMART Social Media Is Sustainable

Let's face it. Social media does have a "flash in the pan" reputation. Why would I want to spend any time putting together a social media marketing plan when social media won't be around in ten, or even five years? Social media as we know it may fade, but as long as authors write books, they will need to use some form of marketing to get them into the hands of readers.

We need a marketing system that will endure through many cycles of fads and will flow seamlessly with whatever new technology or cultural trends emerge next. In order to use social media effectively, we need to build a base of sustainable marketing practices that we can apply to any type of media over time.

What Is Sustainable Social Media?

Sustainable practices ensure that your marketing efforts will stand the test of time and continue to produce success regardless of whether Facebook or Twitter disappear from the internet. Sustainable marketing practices are about using goals, objectives, strategies, and tactics to build fundamental practices that can prevail against the winds of business and cultural change. These practices include building a loyal audience that will buy your books, strategies that revitalize and promote books on your back list, and content that provides value and connection to your most influential fans. These are practices that are built to last.

10 Characteristics of Sustainable Social Media

Sustainable social media marketing has ten clear characteristics that act as a filter for every plan we make, every strategy we implement, and every tool we pull out of the tool box. Use these ten characteristics to guide your planning process.

1. Sustainable social media is organic. Organic practices are ethical. They rely on natural growth and grassroots movements. They are fed by word of mouth, shares, and likes. The audience decides if the product fits their needs. If it does, they spread the word and your message grows.

If your marketing is not organic, you may have growth, but it will be temporary. Examples of inorganic marketing practices are buying social media followers, buying book reviews, paying for tweets or retweets, and many others. They are forced growth strategies that do not build a sustainable following.

Paid advertising can spur organic growth. These practices include buying Facebook ads to build a mailing list, buying book cover space on a review blog, taking out an ad in the newspaper, joining an author service that promotes your books (as long as they promote them ethically), or buying a BookBub ad, to name a few. Not all these will work for you, and you'll have to learn which paid alternatives bring returns.

2. Sustainable social media values diversity. Your potential readers are diverse. Your marketing message has to connect with many different segments and marketing efforts need to be specialized to serve those segments.

For instance, you may write to a large age demographic. Older generations of readers use different social media than 18-year-olds do. People also use Facebook for different reasons than they use Twitter or Pinterest, so you cannot assume that "copy and paste" will connect with everyone. All content is not created equal because all audiences are not created equal.

3. Sustainable social media adds value. When Jay Baer first wrote *Youtility* in 2013, his message was revolutionary. The subtitle of the book is, "Why smart marketing is about help, not hype." The definition of Youtility:

"Youtility is marketing that's wanted by customers. Youtility is massively useful information, provided for free, that creates long-term trust and kinship between your brand and your customers."

In the book, Baer talks about the fundamental shift in consumer buying habits that has "altered the success formula for businesses". People no longer respond to interruptive marketing that coerces them in buying. In his new book, *The New Rules Of Sales And Service*, David Meerman Scott talks about the same shift, saying that instead of selling to people, we need to help them to buy. Baer says, "in this climate, Youtility is not an option; it's necessary." SMART social media marketing adds value and wins permission to sell. You can't add value by screaming, "Buy my book!" But you can earn the right to ask them to buy with content that adds value and meets a need.

4. Sustainable social media builds loyalty. When you put your readers' needs before your own, you build loyalty. Your need is to sell, but if that comes across as your primary motive in content, people will turn a deaf ear. A loyal fan is worth multiple book sales, and it takes less time and money to sell to someone who has already bought. That is a primary tenet of marketing.

5. Sustainable social media starts in a local community. The base of a successful social media starts with a core group of invested fans. These are people with a first-degree connection to you whether they are reviewers, a Facebook group, newsletter subscribers, a book club, avid readers, or friends. When you make a connection with people, there is a level of reciprocal obligation that is triggered. You will need to build a community of real people. You may not know them all personally, but they will have your back and buy your books. You will not have long-term success without a community.

6. Sustainable social media uses your community's knowledge and strengths. Once you build that strong community, let them in.

Give them a chance to vote on covers or name a character. Crowdsource. Ask them what other authors they love to read, and publish their recommendations in your newsletter. Enlist their help to launch your new books.

Rob Fugetta's company, Zuberance, helps brands "turn enthusiastic customers into a powerful marketing force". In his book *Brand Advocates,* he revealed that their research found that 49 percent of Advocates listed a good experience with a brand as the primary reason why they recommend. The second biggest motivation was to help others. In Chapter 11 we'll talk about how to find and empower those advocates.

7. Sustainable social media earns trust. Way back when in social media history (2008), Seth Godin wrote a seminal book called *Permission Marketing.* Permission marketing is the opposite of interruptive marketing. A good example of interruptive marketing is a television commercial or an annoying pop-up on a website that has no connection to the website content. In his book, Godin stressed that brands need to make a friend before they can make a customer. He stressed the importance of shaping a message so people will accept it rather than just throwing it out there and seeing if it sticks. Chris Brogan and Julien Smith continued this line of thought in the book *Trust Agents*. The authors contend that today's consumers are cynical, savvy, and informed. Successful marketing is built on a base of transparency. People have highly sophisticated bullshit detectors today and trust their friends much more than they trust advertisers. Be a friend.

We all have a list of people that we wholeheartedly give permission to sell to us. Michael Hyatt is on my list. He can send me as many emails as he likes promoting a new course or book because over the years he has given me so much valuable content for free (webinars, video courses, daily blog pieces, ebooks) that I trust him. He has solved problems for me, helped me to be better organized, and made me a better writer—all for free. Yes, I have purchased courses from him. But I am not annoyed if he sends me five or six emails in a week promoting a new course I am not interested in. I just delete them. He has earned my permission to sell.

8. Sustainable social media starts with a plan. Franklin Delano Roosevelt said, "In politics, nothing happens by accident. If it happens, you can bet it was planned that way." The same can be said about marketing or any kind of business success. Top brands aren't flying by the seat of their pants. Marketing without a plan is like playing darts blindfolded (a favorite saying of mine that will pop up occasionally). You can get close, but if you hit the bull's-eye, you don't know how you got there and probably can't replicate it again. That plan doesn't need to be a multi-page document or a series of complicated spreadsheets. But we need a plan.

9. Sustainable social media can be integrated seamlessly with other forms of marketing. Traditional marketing (magazines, newspaper, radio, direct mail, television) and social media work well together. Branding (both visual and message) plays a big part in this partnership. When your fans go to your website, they should feel the same vibe (message-wise and visually) that they feel on your Facebook page or in your print materials. They should be able to recognize you wherever you are.

10. Sustainable social media marketing honors both innovation and strategy. One of the toughest things in social media is to separate strategy from innovation. One of the core values of true innovation is failure. Very few inventors get it right the first time. If Thomas Edison didn't believe in failure, we would all still be sitting in the dark with candles.

But we can't market with innovation alone. When it comes to marketing, we lower the odds of failure by using principles that are already proven. Within that framework, there is plenty of room for innovation. But, if you are just marketing by trying every new thing that comes along, you will fail.

Action Steps

1. What characteristics of sustainable social media resonate with you? Why?

2. How do you think authors can deliver more help and less hype in their social media marketing?

Chapter 3: SMART Social Media Is Manageable

Do the math. There are 24 hours in a day—1440 minutes or 86,400 seconds. However you count your time, you will never have more. Insert writing, maybe a second job, a spouse, children, social events, eating, exercising, sleeping, watching TV, and going online. I am exhausted already. How is a writer supposed to find time to market books, much less figure out how to use social media for marketing? Making social media marketing manageable is about learning how to take inventory of your time, resources, skill, and comfort level, and then plan accordingly.

Manage Your Time - Don't Let It Manage You

None of us can control how much time is in a day, but we can control how we use it. Efficiency and organization are your friends. There are endless tools, apps, and systems out there to help you organize your time better. The key is to find one that works for you. I have tried many, ditched many, and kept only a few. One of the problems I find with tools is that people suffer from FOMO—fear of missing out—so they want to try everything that comes along, constantly looking for a better way. My advice is that if a tool works, use it. Something better will always come along, but you may not need something better. Here are some of the characteristics I look for in a good organizational tool and some recommendations:

1. **Free.** I am cheap. I can't always find something that does the job for free, but it's always my first option. I am not opposed to paying for a tool if it is the best option and it fits in my budget, but that is not my norm. I have to work within a budget so I am picky.

2. **Accomplishes more than one task.** I love that tools that do many things. Evernote is a good example. I use it for a lot of tasks and it is free. I can put it on every device I have. I just happened to

start using it when it first came out, and I see no reason to change now because it keeps evolving. I know there might be better tools out there, but knowing that learning a new tool takes valuable time, I stick with what works until it doesn't work anymore. Another tool that accomplishes more than one task for me is Sprout Social. It is a multi-purpose social media tool for posting, reporting, scheduling, search, listening, and much more. It is similar to Buffer. Both these tools (and others in their price range) have multiple functions and can save you time. If your social media presence consists solely of Facebook, you don't need either. These tools are a step above a Hootsuite or TweetDeck, which both have good free versions but not as many functions. If your goals are simple and you don't need the bells and whistles, their free versions might be good for you.

3. **Saves me time.** I use one tool to post on social media—just one. I like tools that let me accomplish multiple tasks in one location because they save time. We are inundated with a constant parade of new social media tools, so beware of FOMO. It's a distraction and a time waster. Find tools that help you reach your goals and stick with them. Always remember the time investment on the learning curve.

4. **Simple to use.** I use Excel spreadsheets for many tasks—reviewer databases, publishing schedules, contact information. I use my Google Calendar as an editorial calendar. I use Kanban Flow (free version) to keep my day on track. These are all standalone tools I use to be more organized, but each can perform many tasks. I use Toggl because I have to track a virtual assistant. My time is valuable and I don't want to take time to learn complex systems when simple will do.

5. **Shareable.** Someday there will come a time, if it hasn't come already, that you will need to collaborate on a project or share a file. I use Dropbox religiously. But I have a client who insists on using Google Drive, so I use that too. If you use Chrome for your internet browser, Google Drive is easy to set up.

As you can probably tell I like time-saving tools. But I don't take on any more than I need. I have two pieces of advice: find something you like and keep using it until it doesn't work anymore. New isn't always better. Second, look for free first.

Final thoughts: tools can be distractions that waste more time than they are worth. Guard your time carefully when it comes to learning a flashy new organizational tool. If a pad of paper with today's list of tasks is your go-to, more power to you. Do what works. You'll have less anxiety in the end and likely produce more and better books.

How Much Time Is Enough?

You may need a lifestyle change to make the best use of your time on social media. It is too easy to get distracted if you also use social media for personal entertainment. Even though social media marketing is an endeavor that you plug in to your list of writing tasks, personal social media time is not. Separate business from pleasure. The first rule of thumb to make social media manageable is to make it part of your author routine. Then, the amount of time you spend on it every day will be determined by your master plan.

There are four types of social media marketing tasks that require different portions of the time you dedicate to marketing as a whole. The time allotments I suggest are only a guideline to demonstrate their importance. Your social media marketing time should include all four.

1. Research: Before you make a decision to start a new social media platform, redesign a website, start an email newsletter, or learn a new piece of software, you need to do research on whether the product or task is a good fit for your goals. This is where good resources will cut your research time significantly (see Chapter 20 on SMART Resources). Research is a task. Once you get good at researching, you will know when you reach the tipping point of information to make a good decision and move on to the next task.

Research should not take more than 10 percent of your marketing time. But it is a necessary task. We're not talking research for your writing here, we're talking marketing research only. ==I use an RSS reader and Google search for this task==. Also, reading books on marketing and listening to podcasts falls in this category as well.

2. Learning: Whenever you are learning a new task such as setting up a new social media channel, redesigning a website, or learning a new email application, you will need to allocate learning time. The amount of time will depend on the task. Don't try and redesign your website all in one day or learn Scrivener in one sitting. Divide the time for these tasks over days or weeks. I guarantee you'll never quit learning.

Don't let learning cut into your other tasks. There are some exceptions when you'll need to spend more time learning than usual, such as learning a new website content management system, but don't get bogged down. Move on after an hour. Start again tomorrow. If learning starts to suck too much time, find some resources to help cut the learning curve like free webinars or blog articles. Learning should only take about 10-15 percent of your total time because you will do it in spurts.

3. Editorial tasks: Writing posts and scheduling, making images, writing blog pieces, finding images, putting together video, taking photos, pinning—these are all editorial tasks. This is the bulk of your time, which will probably work out to 45 percent or more.

4. Monitoring and connecting: You can't be successful by just posting on social media and forgetting about it. That is called broadcasting and it is extremely ineffective and a huge turn-off to fans. The very thought of connecting with fans strikes fear into many authors, but it is a necessary task of SMART social media marketing. You may think that this is editorial, but it isn't.

Connecting is responding. It is liking fan comments, it is answering questions, it is thanking people for reviews, it is asking a question prompted by a fan comment to continue the group conversation, it is retweeting, it is liking other people's pins, it is answering blog comments. I'm not saying you need to be active on all of the above channels, but you get the idea. Whatever social media channels you use, be present in those conversations.

This is where relationships are formed. This is the "social" in "social media". It might be uncomfortable at first, but just be yourself. If you build the community, they will come. Start with 20 percent of your marketing time here.

5. Evaluation: Periodically, you should revisit your marketing goals, look at your objectives, and see if your invested time is getting any return. We'll talk more about how to do that in Chapter 7. Spend ten percent of your marketing time every week doing this. I allocate a chunk of time to this every Saturday or Sunday.

These time percentages are a starting point so you can get an idea of how time-consuming each task should be in your marketing plan. I like to think of the time in weekly allotments because you probably won't do them all every day.

The Replacement Theory

To make your social media marketing manageable, start by taking an inventory of your resources. One of the biggest mistakes I see people make is taking on tasks that they don't have the resources for. So start with an inventory of your time, money, connections, and tools.

Time is finite. Nobody gets more than 24 hours. So how do you make the best use of what you have? That starts with three things: prioritizing, organizing, and culling. We are not all wired to be systematic. Your definition of organization might be different than mine. My writer-daughter says I am anal about organization. That is who I am. I am also strategic. Consequently, it is easier for me to design systems that help me get organized. But I know everyone doesn't have that focus.

So let's start with a universal understanding. The first step in organizing your time, no matter what your personality, is being aware of how you use your time currently. For instance, if you currently don't have any time allocated for marketing tasks, you'll have to figure out how much time you can pull or save from other tasks to start. Could you get up a half hour earlier everyday or go to bed a half hour later? Your marketing time doesn't need to be inserted there, but it gives your schedule flexibility. To add a behavior to your already busy day, you're going to have to make some changes. Don't make the mistake of just adding more tasks without taking anything away or consolidating others.

I've always had two wardrobes: my work wardrobe and my leisure wardrobe. When we first moved to our current town, we lived in a rental while we were looking to buy a home. All of a sudden I was faced with a reality: I had more clothes than my closet would hold. Not only that, I discovered I had way more clothes than I needed. To solve the problem, I decided to give away anything that I hadn't worn several times in the last year. I always hated to throw things out. You never know when you might need those stirrup pants again, right? As a result of the culling process, I adopted a new clothes buying strategy I call the "replacement theory" which guarantees my closet will never grow. If I ever buy anything new, I have to give away something I already have. That goes for shoes, jewelry, t-shirts, whatever. It also makes me more hesitant to add anything.

Along with organizing your time, you might consider learning how to multitask your social media marketing. Sandra Beckwith, one of my favorite bloggers on book marketing (Build Book Buzz) wrote a great piece called "7 Ways To Promote Your Book While Watching TV" that can start your wheels turning about how to find time for some of your book marketing tasks. Waiting rooms are great places to do research. So is waiting in the car to pick up your kids after school. Do some brainstorming. How can you better use your time? Don't just pile it on. Remember the replacement theory.

Time Is Money

Before we can talk about money, we have to bust a myth: *social media is not free*. Believing that is a recipe for frustration and failure. It's true that some of the tools are free, but our time is worth something. If you write books, you know that. My writer-daughter has an interesting piece of software that lets her input her time on tasks, how much money she spends on various stages of the book by category, and then calculates exactly what her time is worth. It is a reminder that every minute we spend working is worth something. We might not get a good return on all our time up front, but it is still has a tangible value.

For instance, what if you had to pay someone to put up a Facebook page? That can cost you anywhere from $50 to $200 (or more) depending on how complicated it is; landing pages, links to newsletters, stores, and other social media, images, etc. Then add the ongoing cost of paying someone to manage it for you if you either can't or don't want to. For a couple of posts a day, graphics, and engagement, that may cost you another hundred a month or more depending on what all is involved. (Just an aside: I don't recommend doing any of the above because I believe that with a minimal amount of training, anyone can build a pretty engaging Facebook presence with a small time investment.)

There are, however, some things that are worth spending money on. Think of it like you would a book cover. Sure, you can make your own covers, but unless you're a graphic designer, you may end up on Book Binge's WTF Cover Saturday feature. Because a good cover may be the single most important feature in attracting new readers, you have to think about its worth.

Sometimes you can find necessary services for free. I know people like Constant Contact or AWeber for newsletters, but you can get a subscription to MailChimp for free until you exceed the subscriber limit. That gives you a chance to learn how to do it well without spending any money— fewer bells and whistles, but enough to learn.

When it comes to paid services, balance your time against the worth of the task. You may want to buy images to use in branding materials such as cover photos or image quotes, or you may want to make your own on Canva for free. I wouldn't hire anybody to do something I can do well myself with a little training, but graphic design and the need for professional images changes the decision process. I buy images on iStockphoto or Shutterstock for PowerPoint presentations and branding materials, but I make my own images in Canva for blog posts and cover photos on social media channels. I am confident in my ability to produce quality in some areas, but not in areas where my lack of skills would be evident.

Do I Really Need a Budget?

The short answer is yes. Everything you do related to your business should have a budget. The long answer is you'll have to figure out what, if anything, you are going to budget for as you go along. But you can definitely get along with mostly free to begin your SMART social media marketing plan. Just remember that your time is worth something, so use it wisely.

Other Resources at Your Disposal

Money isn't the only resource you have at your disposal:

1. Professional connections: Your network of author friends can be an important resource. Joining author organizations, local writer's groups, and forums will help you build relationships that can be a helpful source of information.

2. Virtual connections: You should be using social media to do more than connect with fans. Follow other authors and book marketers on social media, join author Facebook groups, or join forums. You never know where and when your virtual connections will be a resource with a big return. Pay it forward, be generous, and share what you can to help other authors be successful.

3. Social media blogs, ebooks, and podcasts: We'll cover this more in depth in Chapter 20, but know that there is a lot of good free information out there to help you become a better marketer.

4. Paid subscription services: Author services like Jim Kukral's Author Marketing Club (I am a member) can provide resources that would take a lot of time and money to find. Kukral has a reasonably priced paid tool that offers many services to indie authors including a book reviewer database, a book description template, a stable of how-to videos, free book promotion services and more.

Passion + Skill = Success

Not long ago I took on a client as a favor to a friend. She was a good writer but her online presence was a mess. As a result, her discoverability score was almost zero. She had two Facebook pages that were somehow intertwined. She had bought a website package from GoDaddy but had lost interest in it when the content management system got too complicated. I helped her clean up her Facebook pages, got her a simple website built on WordPress, and put her on a schedule to post on Facebook. She is collecting email addresses on her website and hopes to tackle a newsletter sometime in the future. It's a start. Sad to say, I don't think she is an outlier.

A social media presence is a must-have for authors. Why? As social media channels have started showing up in search engines, social media has surpassed web searching as the number one source of internet referral traffic. You can have passion about your writing and write great books. But the truth is, the majority of indie authors need to market their own books. Stephen King may not need social media marketing (although he's great on Twitter), but you do.

Being a SMART social media marketer is about more than slapping up a Facebook page and posting every time you release a new book. To be successful as a writer takes skill development and work. The same is true of marketing. You may want to argue that if you write good books, people will buy them. Maybe, maybe not. Amazon has more to say about that than you do. But SMART social media marketing can differentiate you from all the other noise out there and build a platform that keeps you in front of fans when Amazon doesn't choose to promote your books.

So where is your current skill level? Can you manage your own website? Make your own cover photos for social media channels? Can you put together an engaging newsletter? Take inventory of your current skill level. When it comes time to put a plan together in Chapter 7, you'll have to keep your skill level in mind. Your plan needs to be customized for you. That is what keeps it manageable.

Your Comfort Level

In my early days, I was a high school teacher and coach. I am a strong believer in strength training to improve athletic performance, but not just any training. You can't send a basketball player to the weight room and have them do bench presses for an hour. You have to design a program specific to developing strength for the tasks needed for the sport: quickness, speed, muscle endurance.

Strength training relies on stress. Strength coaches use formulaic programs to put just enough stress on the muscles to increase strength for the desired performance. Too much stress causes injury.

Your growth as a SMART social media marketer will require some stress, some discomfort. But it would be a failure to push you out into the social media fast lane with a list of platforms and tasks to do that are too far beyond your comfort zone. You'll get discouraged and lose heart.

Start at square one. Educate yourself. Don't listen to people who say you have to be on every social media channel to be successful, or that you have to blog, or have to be on Twitter, or that you need a Pinterest channel. You may love to do those things eventually. But they may scare you to death right now. Start where you are comfortable. In Part Three of this book we'll talk about the toolbox. We'll approach it with purpose, but we'll start slow. Your comfort level is an important aspect of making SMART social media marketing manageable, but you should always be striving to know more and be better at it. After all, the ultimate goal is to sell more books and build a bigger base of loyal fans.

Of all the characteristics of SMART social media marketing, this is the one that is most often missing. Peer pressure, lack of good information, and just plain naiveté push many an author into a situation where social media marketing becomes unmanageable. Start right. Do it on your terms, but do it with the best information you can find from the best sources. Count the cost before you dive in. If time management is a trap for you, I recommend getting some good resources and considering some lifestyle changes. Poor time management will kill your passion quicker than anything.

Action Steps

1. How much time, on average, do you spend everyday working on marketing your author brand and your books? Do you think it is too much or not enough?
2. Jot down some thoughts on how you could structure your days differently to carve out a little more time for marketing tasks.

Chapter 4: SMART Social Media Is Audience-Specific

"Audience is not brought to you or given to you; it's something that you fight for. You can forget that, especially if you've had some success." - Bruce Springsteen

Social media marketing functions best when the audience dictates platform and message. Today, much of our marketing efforts are backwards. We think a platform will deliver an audience, but a platform just delivers a message to an audience we have already built. Your audience is a critical asset. And I don't mean the general audience you are writing for, but the audience you have grown and engaged on social media—your proprietary audience.

Building a Proprietary Audience

We have three types of marketing media at our disposal: **paid** (advertisements, affiliate marketing, or anything you pay for), **owned** (website, social media channels, catalogs, blog, email), and **earned** (mentions, shares, reviews, feature articles, guest blogs). These are all channels we use to connect with our audience.

In his book *Audience*, Jeffrey Rohrs says we fail to develop an audience because we are focused on channel development. We have channel strategies but not audience strategies. Rohrs implores readers to embrace what he calls The Audience Imperative:

"Use your paid, owned, and earned media not only to sell in the short term, but also to increase the size, engagement, and value of your proprietary audience over the long term."

SMART social media marketing has two purposes: develop a loyal proprietary audience and sell books.

One Audience ... Many Faces

Your proprietary audience is made up of many parts or segments of people. They have different motivations for being there, different buying habits, and are in need of different information. Rohrs explains:

- **Seekers** are looking for something of personal interest. You gain them by giving them the kind of relevant content they are looking for. They are usually not ready for personal contact. They are seeking information, not connection.
- **Amplifiers** are looking for content as well, but for their own audiences. They will magnify the reach of your content by sharing it with a motive of gaining credibility or helping their own audience. These are often reporters, influencers, advocates, consultants, reviewers, and bloggers.
- **Joiners** are your most valuable asset, according to Rohrs. They are the foundation of your audience because they respond to your calls to action whether those are subscribe, follow, pin, register, join, or buy. They willingly give up their personal information for value. They volunteer to be marketed to.

Audiences crave relevant content: the right message at the right time delivered on the right channel that meets a personal need. Let's unpack effective ways that you can provide that content to your audience.

The Right Message

Make sure your content includes messages to all segments of your audience. If you only address the joiners, you will intimidate the seekers. Publish a variety of content types aimed at each audience while being sensitive to the amount of selling you do. We will address this further in Chapter 10.

You can use calls to action in every type of message. Just remember that seekers are only looking for information. The more you give them, the more likely it is they will take the next step to sharing. Messages have to add value to be relevant, however. Rohrs offers these five "Red Velvet" principles to add value to your audience members:
1. Serve the individual. Marketing is about customer service.
2. Honor their unique preferences.
3. Deliver them timely, relevant content that makes their lives better.
4. Surprise them with unexpected access. Take down the rope that holds them back.
5. Delight them with your humanity.

The Right Stuff

Social media channels have unique cultures. Posting the same verbatim message to multiple channels is considered lazy marketing by your audience. You need to educate yourself about the different channel cultures and user behaviors to make sure you are posting the right message to the right people. I'll cover this in depth in Chapter 10, but for now just know that each channel has unwritten rules of behavior. Gone are the days when social media marketing meant posting one message to every social media channel.

The purpose of matching the right message with the right channel at the right time to the right person is to get noticed and remembered. All of us are struggling for the precious commodity of sustainable attention. Viral videos will not do that. Screaming "Buy my book" on Twitter will not do that.

Treating Your Audience Like Friends

When Seth Godin wrote his book *Permission Marketing* in 1999, the core concept of "turning strangers into friends and friends into customers" was a revolutionary concept.

According to Godin, "Permission marketing is the privilege (not the right) of delivering anticipated, personal, and relevant messages to people who actually want to get them. It recognizes that consumers have the power to ignore marketing. It realizes that treating people with respect is the best way to earn their attention." Basically, it is the bedrock of how marketing works today. His theory was based on the idea that people started to challenge the concept that marketing was about selling them something, not helping them solve a real problem. They found that they could gather their own information on products and services and make informed decisions to buy.

Chris Brogan and Julien Smith picked up this ball in 2009 and wrote the book *Trust Agents,* which was based on the same thesis but applied to marketing on the web. Brogan walked the talk building a huge audience of loyal fans based on the principle of giving without receiving. He found the balance between giving value and selling by giving fans "my best work" and reminding them he was going to sell on occasion. After years of being on the receiving end of his valuable free content, he has earned the right to sell to me. Because I trust him, I don't feel the pressure to buy things I don't need.

How can you make friends out of strangers? Start by revisiting the Red Velvet principles mentioned earlier. If you want to make friends out of strangers you have to work at it. Social media marketing will bring you a return in the long run if you learn to value your fans. There is no shortcut to building a loyal audience.

Finding Out More About Your Audience

Does the phrase "audience research" freak you out? It will be tougher to find the right marketing strategy for your audience if you don't know who they are. There are many ways to do audience research without getting a marketing degree, breaking the bank, or poring over columns of figures. In Chapter 8, I'll give you a wealth of information on how to do simple audience research that will help you focus your social media marketing efforts on the right people.

Action Steps

1. Are you a seeker, an amplifier, or a joiner on social media? Maybe a hybrid? How do you exhibit those behaviors as a fan or follower?

2. Do you have an idea what your proprietary audience looks like? Jot down a few characteristics of your typical audience member.

Chapter 5: SMART Social Media Is Relevant

We often confuse relevance with creativity. Relevance is not about being cutting edge or joining the latest fad. Relevant social media delivers the right message to the right person at the right time through the right channel. Sometimes it is easier to understand relevance by looking at our common misconceptions.

Relevance Is Not…

1. Relevance isn't about tools. Tools come and go, and if you are relying on Facebook or Snapchat (heaven forbid) to bring you success, you are on the wrong train. Tools deliver the relevant information. Tools help you target the audience you need with engaging content that will help them buy.

2. Relevance isn't about being hip or on the cutting edge. A first cousin to number one, being cool doesn't meet your buyers' needs. Engagement isn't about being an early adopter. If your mantra is "sell, sell, sell", it will sound just as hollow on the latest social media channel as it does on Facebook. The channel is not the message; choose the channel to match the message.

3. Relevance doesn't always increase with reach. Reach is a measurement of how far your social media message goes. It's about eyeballs—how many people see your post. You can fake reach by purchasing one of those silly retweet packages for $15, but those are a waste of money because the tweets are not targeted at your book buyers. The followers on those sites are random people—mostly people they have acquired by following accounts that automatically follow back or by just buying followers. Your readers are not following these fly-by-night sites so who cares how many times they tweet, "Buy this book." Save your money, do your own tweeting and solicit the help of your loyal fans to spread your messages.

4. Relevance doesn't increase by being on every social media channel. More isn't better on social media. It's all about audience behavior. Where are your readers and where are they in the habit of buying? Targeted is better. Know your audience.

Relevance Is About the Strength of Relationships

In information science, relevance is the way in which one topic is related to another. Google search algorithms rely on relevance to show you exactly what you are searching for based on a number of behaviors. If you Google the phrase "*social media marketing*", for instance, an algorithm will search for pages that others have referenced on the subject in addition to other relevance measurements. The order of web pages you see in the results is carefully selected based on your past searches, where you go on the web, and where others have gone as well. So each page is assigned a relevance score, if you will.

I used to watch a game show in the eighties called Match Game. Contestants and celebrities were asked a fill-in-the-blank question and the contestant who could match the answer of the highest number of celebrities won the round.

Relevance is somewhat like the Match Game. It's a matter of matching content to a specific audience. Based on your audience research, you match your content with their buying and reading habits. The degree to which you connect with their needs and habits, the more relevant your content is.

Facebook uses a relevance score for their ads that determines which ads will be seen and how much they will cost. The better you are at matching your product and message to the targeted audience, the higher your score is and the more likely it is that Facebook will show your ad to users. You may think that is unfair, but actually it is a consumer-friendly algorithm. Facebook users complained for years that Facebook was full of spammy ads, especially in their news feeds. Facebook made a promise to users to show them only ads they would be interested in, matching the products with their age, interests, location, and user habits (other products and pages they had liked). And it's actually a good deal for advertisers as well. The more I know my audience, the better I can target them. Another benefit for a high relevance score on Facebook is that your ads cost less.

What Is Relevance in Social Media?

These relevance calculations from both Google and Facebook give us an idea of just how important relevance is in social media marketing. There are four factors you need to consider to be relevant in social media.

1. **Who** is in your audience? And don't say "everyone". We're not talking about outliers or small percentage groups, we're talking majority demographics. If you write young adult books, you are targeting young people ages 10-18, generally speaking. So your social media has to be aimed at that age group. Also, parents buy a lot of the books for the younger end of that spread so you will want to reach them as well. If you write romance, generally you are not writing for men. What are your readers' interests? Gather basic demographics.

2. **What** other authors write books like mine? Knowing what authors write books that are similar to yours can help you in the hunt for an audience for your books. Have you liked the Facebook pages of other authors like you? Followed them on Twitter or Pinterest? Read any of their books? It is especially helpful to keep an eye on how they market.

I have one client who routinely asks her Facebook fans to recommend books by other authors. It's foolish to think your fans are only reading your books. Do some research. Also, becoming familiar with other authors' audiences can help when it comes to buying ads on social media where a like author's audience is an option for targeting an ad.

3. **Where** are your readers? Once you know who your readers are, it's time to find out where they are. Pew Internet Research (www.pewinternet.org) is an excellent source of data on social media use. There are also a lot of "studies" available online, but you have to be careful of the reliability of their data. Some companies commission research studies that favor their products to use as marketing. That doesn't mean their data is bad, it just means it might be skewed as a sales tool. Pew Internet Research is a nonprofit organization that publishes all their data for free, and they are reliable. I follow their Internet And Tech blog to make sure I keep up.

4. **When** are readers online and when are they buying books? It is extremely helpful to have data on when your audience is more likely to purchase books. These are the times you ramp up your selling. It helps you to develop a better mix of helping to selling. There is abundant data from HubSpot and others about what times of the day and week certain demographic groups are online. One of my favorite books on this subject is called *The Science Of Marketing* by Dan Zarella. HubSpot and Buffer publish studies along these lines occasionally as well. I've written much more on this subject in Chapters 8 and 9.

5. **Why** should your readers care? Why should they buy your book? Defining what makes your book valuable to readers is gold. A great example of this is the book descriptions on Amazon. In addition to your cover, it's one of the main motivators for buying your book, especially for new readers. It must move the reader to want to know more about your book. Good copywriting is an art and

can be learned. Attention spans today are shorter and more discerning than ever before. Readers are bombarded with so many messages that they quickly move on if you don't hook them.

Action Steps

1. Using the relevance measures discussed in this chapter, how relevant do you think your social media content is to your audience?

2. Which social media channels do you think are most relevant to your audience? Do you have an active presence there now?

3. If you have a Facebook page in addition to your profile, go and look at the last ten posts you made on your author page and ask yourself, "Why would my readers care about each one of these?"

Chapter 6: SMART Social Media Means Tactics Last, Strategy First

Every summer when I was a kid, my mom piled us all in the car and we drove six hours to our grandparents' cabin on a lake in northern Wisconsin for weeks of fun-filled fishing, swimming, catching frogs, eating fresh strawberries, following deer tracks, reading books, and playing ring toss. It was heaven for a kid. What we didn't know at the time was that drive was a bit of a nightmare for my mother. Six hours in a car with three little kids, no air conditioner, no cell phones, no McDonald's, and no freeways with lovely rest areas every 50 miles. It was a challenge. But she had a plan.

My mom never studied business or probably didn't know that goals have to be measurable, but she knew innately that getting through six hours with three kids in a car required a game plan with goals, objectives, strategy, and tactics. She had every 60 miles strategically mapped out from snacks to games to stops. My mom knew where every picnic table and tourist attraction was on that 300-mile stretch. She knew every public bathroom, every drive-in, and every city park. I really didn't come to appreciate my mom's strategic brilliance when it came to road trips until I had two kids of my own. It takes a plan to manage kids in a car over hundreds of miles and come out with your sanity on the other end.

Your marketing will never reach its full potential unless you understand the importance of strategy. And strategy is not having a schedule to tweet something every hour on the hour. You can do that, but it isn't strategic unless it's a function of reaching a specific goal. It's a tactic. And the biggest mistake we make in marketing is implementing tactics without a plan.

The Difference Between Strategy and Tactics

Sometimes people have a hard time distinguishing between strategy and tactics. I think that's because tactics are tasks and strategy is the why behind the task. Many people don't think ask themselves, *why am I doing this*? If you don't start with the why, you won't be able to connect your goals to your tactics. You may have a laundry list of things to do on social media, but you may not have a clue what they are going to actually accomplish.

When you use SMART social media marketing strategy, you get more results in less time. You will have a plan that makes the best use of your time, resources, and skills to reach your goals witnessed by measures of success you have predetermined. And you will understand fully how your website, newsletter, and social media marketing are all connected and how they work together.

Some authors using social media for marketing express differing thoughts. Some claim that nobody can sell books on social media and some claim they can make a living selling books on Twitter. Neither statement understands the power of SMART social media marketing to build deeper connections with fans faster than any other form of marketing out there. But marketing success does not come with social media alone. Social media is not a magic pill.

But just saying you have strategy doesn't bring automatic success either. Some people's strategy is flawed, and the results will reflect that. Workarounds like tweet blasters and buying Facebook fans are unethical and just plain stupid. Strategic marketing is based on simple growth principles, not schemes.

I like to use the illustration of Google Maps to explain. When you punch in a starting point and a destination in Google Maps, the application generates a line between the two. That is your strategy—a road map of how to accomplish the goal of getting to your destination. When you scroll down in the map results, you'll see a blow-by-blow report of how to get there: take Highway 15 for three miles, turn left on exit 234, then turn right on Front Street, and so forth. Those directions are your tactics. Some directions take only a minute to fulfill, others take hours. Those directions are nonexistent without a beginning point and a destination.

Start With Strategy

Let me just say up front that the idea of strategy should not be intimidating. Anyone can succeed with SMART social media marketing. You don't need a business degree or need to be a marketing professional to get it. Strategic marketing is just a map you put together. The recipe is tried and true, and it is user-friendly. You don't have to reinvent the wheel, just plug in your ingredients.

The scope of your strategic plan is up to you. Whether your plan is one page or 10 pages, it needs to start with the same four pieces: ==goals, objectives, strategies, and tactic==s. In the next part of the book on fundamentals, we'll take a closer look at what strategy means for book marketing and how it will set you on the path to success.

Action Steps

1. How do you react to the statement that Facebook is not a strategy but a tactic? Does it
   make sense to you?
2. Can you name a couple of strategies you are trying to accomplish with your
   marketing?
3. So, what are some of the tactics that are helping you succeed?

Part II - SMART Fundamentals

In sports we teach successful performance through the breakdown of fundamentals. Great basketball players grew up learning the basics of ball handling, dribbling, footwork, passing, shooting, and one-on-one defense. Social media marketing is no different. Before you can put it all together, you need to learn the fundamentals. Skipping this step might get you some short-term success, but your marketing will never reach its full potential.

Chapter 7: The Plan - Start With GOST

I learned to sew on a machine in middle school. My mother had a sewing machine so I was glad to have an inexpensive way to add some variety to my closet. One thing I learned quickly: the fastest and easiest way to sew a garment that fit was to use a pattern. Simplicity, the biggest pattern maker, had a huge catalog of patterns I would pore through at the J.C. Penney fabric department. I had a group of like-sized friends that shared patterns. The great thing about sewing according to a pattern was that you could change the material, the buttons, or the style of sleeves and you would have an entirely different garment than your friends. One pattern, many variations.

In marketing, success also starts with a pattern. It doesn't matter how many social media channels you have, or whether you want to buy advertisements, your plan relies on a pattern or template that has four key elements: goals, objectives, strategies, and tactics, or GOST for short. No matter how elementary or complex you want your social media marketing to be, you start with GOST. In this chapter I will give an overview of the process, and then I'll show you a specific example of a GOST plan in the bonus materials that you can sign up for at the end of the book.

Goals First

A goal states what you want to accomplish. What is your target? What is the bigger picture? Many people use the following formula to define what a good goal should look like:

- **Specific:** Goals need to be specific. "I want to be rich" is not a specific goal. "I want to increase the amount of direct book sales from Book X with social media" is specific. If a goal is not specific, you won't be able to measure it or figure out how to hit it.

Engagement needs to be measured by actions (shares, likes), not follower numbers. Follower numbers just measure potential reach.

- **Measurable:** Goals need to have an outcome. What measurement can I use to decide when the goal is reached? Does the measurement fit the goal?
- **Attainable** (or achievable)**:** You need to have the resources or access to reach your goals. These usually include things like money, time, skills, and commitment. Will I need additional resources to reach this objective? If so, how will that affect my strategy?
- **Realistic or relevant:** The biggest failure comes from setting a goal that is not realistic. I may want to lost 50 pounds before my wedding, but if it is in two months, that is neither safe nor realistic. In the same way, having a goal of reaching a 50 percent engagement rate on my Facebook page is not a realistic goal because the average rate is around 10-15 percent and 30 percent is considered stellar. You may have individual posts (such as when you are giving away books) that climb up over 50 percent, but your page engagement rate isn't going to be that high. If it is, please send me a link to your page—I'd love to see how you're doing it!
- **Time-Specific:** a good goal has a beginning and an end.

Your SMART social media marketing plan shouldn't have too many goals. Each goal requires at least one objective, and each objective may have several strategies. Each strategy then has several tactics. If you multiply that all out, it can be a lot. Keep it simple.

You may start with a goal as simple as " increase the total fan base for my books through online marketing including social media." That may be the only goal. I know it sounds general, but you'll see how we implement it as we go. And it's a great place to start.

Objectives Help Measure the Success of Your Goals

The objective is the measurement that shows whether or not you have reached your goal. It must be something you can track and observe. Using our goal above of "increasing the fan base for my books through social media", you may have a few objectives that look like this:

- Increase the number of fans on my Facebook page by (number or percentage) in the next three months.
- Increase my email newsletter list by (number or percentage) in the next three months.
- Build a new Facebook fan group to 250 fans in the next 12 months.

Your objectives are set based on an increase in proportion to the amount of work you are going to put in. For instance, if you currently have 200 Facebook fans and gain them at the rate of two a week you will only have around 250 in three months' time. In order to reach a goal of 750 in three months, you are going to have to implement some specific strategies to increase your numbers. I do believe it is possible to increase follower numbers in a short period of time, but it will require a change in how you presently operate your Facebook page. That is where the strategy comes in.

Strategies Are a Road Map to Meet Your Goals

Strategies are your road map for reaching your objectives. Your strategies will determine your tactics. Start by taking each individual objective and plan out exactly how you are going to get there building on the principles from part one: sustainable, manageable, audience-specific and relevant.

Sample strategies for *increase the number of fans on my Facebook page from 200 to 750 in the next six months*:
- Strategy 1: Reach out to author friends in my genre to develop a Facebook page tour with giveaways on each designed to

increase follower numbers on all our pages. Also helps fulfill Strategy 3.
- Strategy 2: Develop an advocate campaign revolving around a contest that will encourage loyal fans to help boost the numbers by social sharing and recommendations. Also helps fulfill Strategy 3.
- Strategy 3: Run three contests/giveaways in the next six months that distribute prizes each time a follower counts reaches a milestone. Make sure the milestones are low enough so they are easily reached early in the contests to keep interest levels up. For instance, if you are trying to reach 250 new fans, try using milestones of 50 new followers. That equates to a need for five prize packages during the giveaway.

You can see we are starting to drill down into the specifics. Each of these strategies has a recipe or step-by-step process for implementation called tactics.

Tactics Are Your Daily Grind

Tactics are actually the easiest part of GOST. That's why many people default to tactics—they just do stuff. And if that stuff doesn't work, they don't really know why. But when your tactics are a result of an informed process, you only do the stuff that counts.

Let's keep our example going and pick out one strategy: *reach out to author friends in my genre to develop a Facebook page tour.* I've seen these done a couple of different ways—either the whole group over a period of time, or one author each day like a book launch. We'll do the one-day book launch method. This is also based on the premise that you already network with several author friends in your genre. It won't be as easy to do if you just reach out to people you haven't connected with yet.

One tip: it really helps to put your plan on paper, either digitally or by hand. The written plan is a good map to follow and also has a record of steps you are taking in case you need to change the process. This helps you learn lessons for future reference or make adjustments on the fly. Writing out the tactics doesn't take much time and you only need to get as specific as you need to guide your steps. I use an Excel spreadsheet for this step. It's easy to highlight each task as it gets completed.

Sample tactics for Strategy 1: *Reach out to author friends in my genre to develop a Facebook page tour aimed at increasing fan numbers.*

- Map out a five-day stretch to promote your tour at least a month out.
- Reach out to author friends until you find at least four or five who have 500 or more fans each who would like to participate in the project. Agree on a date.
- Come up with a title for your tour you can use in the event promotion, in graphics and in posts.
- Make a list of 2-3 suggested activities to include in each author's "tour destination" such as quizzes, book giveaways, and contests that release prizes based on increased likes.
- Make up a list of posts to promote the tour on all social media channels 7 days prior to the tour. Prepare a save-the-date announcement, preferably with an image that will be posted two weeks out.
- Make up a calendar with every author's time slot and distribute to authors along with guidelines. Ask authors to open their privacy settings to accept posts and pictures from public during the tour. Each author will host their slot on their own Facebook page and the whole tour will begin on your page.
- Explain that you will keep track of time and post on each author's page when it is time to move on to the next page.
- Ask each prospective author to come up with 2-3 inexpensive giveaways for the tour. Every author is responsible for mailing out their own giveaways.
- Make a Facebook event template for each author and have everyone post on their page two weeks out. Have each author's

Facebook page URL and time slot on the event along with giveaways. Make sure to include an image on the event.
- Emphasize the start time and order of pages and what time block each author has.
- Make sure that all authors check in at some time to offer comments on each other's pages during their tour stop.
- Prepare the posts for your own tour stop and take pictures (if applicable) of your giveaways. Ask other authors to promote the tour using their own social media channels.
- Start off the tour on your page. As the guide, offer comments at the beginning and end of each stop and make sure the tour keeps on time.
- If possible, offer one grand prize for the whole tour for a random winner who likes all four pages during the tour.
- Put together a follow-through schedule of posts thanking fans and reminding prize winners to get their contact information to the appropriate author.
- Put together a long-term follow-through calendar of cross-promoting each other's pages over a three-month time period.
- Each author should have a follow-through strategy of exclusive content aimed at the new fans which stretches over a one-month period initially. Get new fans involved with interactive posts, quizzes, polls, picture contests, and other content aimed at soliciting a response.

I use a tactics spreadsheet as a checklist and calendar. Each task needs a deadline of some sort so you know how much time is involved in putting your plan together. This sample helps us see how tactics carry out a strategy. This list may change during the process as you find holes and need to add some tactics. Be thorough and you'll be more successful.

A thorough plan is a social media marketing fundamental. Without one, you are shooting at a target blindfolded. When you sign up to receive the bonus materials at the end of the book, you will receive an extensive planning resource called "Your SMART Social Media Book Launch Plan" that will teach you how to use the

GOST formula to build a successful book launch for any genre and help you apply that formula to all your long- and short-term campaigns.

Action Steps

1. What is one goal you would like to reach with your book marketing? (Hint: make it broad). 2. What are two objectives that define success for that goal? (Again, be specific about how you can measure success)
3. What is one strategy you can use to implement each of those objectives?
4. Write a descriptive paragraph about what tactics should be a part of that strategy.
5. Email me at chris@cksyme.com with your action steps in this chapter. I'd love to see your ideas.

Chapter 8: Know Thy Audience

I used to pick up extra money in college by playing my guitar and singing. My college town had a variety of bars including some strictly for college kids, some for old guys who wanted a quiet place to hang out, and some for middle-aged married couples to socialize and not worry about getting hit on. Each one liked a different kind of music. Consequently, I had to have a repertoire that included rock, pop, country, show music, old folks' songs, and more. To be a hit with each audience, I had to play the kind of music they wanted to hear. I would get booed or fired if I played folk songs in every bar I worked in. But the old guys loved them.

Marketing operates on the same principle. To be a hit with your audience, you have to know them—what they like and dislike, where they buy, what they buy, when they are online, what kind of budget for books they have, and a myriad other pieces of info all based on a demographic base. The better you know your audience, the easier it is to sell to them. You've heard the saying, if you market to everyone, you are marketing to no one. Truth. Sing their songs and they will engage. Play folk songs all night and no matter how well you sing, you will just be background noise.

The Great Audience Disconnect

Nothing is misunderstood like audience. I believe there are several misconceptions we need to address up front that I often hear from authors:

1. I think everybody will like my book. Nope. Not even if you are J.K. Rowling—it ain't gonna happen. There is a reason Amazon lists books by genre. Even though many people read more than one genre, Amazon knows they don't come to the website looking for any old book to read. Sometimes this misconception is just code for, "I don't know who my audience is."

2. If I market to a specific audience, I will limit who will buy my book. There are several factors that will limit the sales of your book, and defining your audience is not one of them. Knowing your audience gives you a specific focus and makes marketing much easier. If every contemporary romance fan out there bought your book, it would be a runaway best seller.

3. I don't believe in marketing. I believe if my book is good, people will buy it. Well, that may be true, but how are readers finding your wonderful book? By osmosis? Amazon won't show it to them unless it is already selling well. You can rely on word of mouth, but that will be a slow build. Many people cite outliers for the "I told you so" of this one. Never make a marketing decision based on an outlier (something that works despite not having the characteristics of success). Some of these are just poorly written books that hit a viral spot with readers. If you want to bank on being an outlier, you may have a long wait.

4. I don't like social media. It's not who I am. Again, that's okay. You don't have to use it to market your books. But consider this: over 40 percent of the world's population is on the internet. According to Internet Live Stats in 2014, almost 87 percent of the U.S. population with internet access was online, including children. Now, add to that data from Pew Internet Research that tells us over 70 percent of adults in the U.S. who use the internet are on Facebook. And 52% of online adults are using more than one social media platform. Why is that data important? Because you need to see how mainstream social media is impacting our everyday lives. That is where people are interacting, where they can discover your book, and tell others how great it is.

A large part of the problem with authors and social media is that much of the marketing hype they see is all about being on every social media platform available. Marketers write countless articles on the latest platforms, telling us all how to get on board or miss the boat. Now don't get me wrong. I love innovation. I love taking risks, but I take risks with new platforms that match my goals. I always tell authors to start slow.

Do Your Research

Audience research can be as simple or complicated as you like.

There is quite a bit of free marketing research available online that tells you who is buying what books where:
- The Publishers Weekly website (http://www.publishersweekly.com/) publishes information about book-buying trends.
- Nielsen's Insights publishes a number of different free research summaries from the entertainment sector. Find them here: http://www.nielsen.com/us/en/insights.html. Use their search function at the top of the page.
- Nielsen publishes an annual report in the early fall sponsored by Bowker and Publishers Weekly called The U.S. Book Consumer Demographics & Buying Behaviors Annual Review. You'll find that many book publishing blogs write commentary about the huge report that costs a whopping $799 to access.
- Kobo Cafe (www.kobocafe.com) also writes blog pieces on who is reading what and where. It's a good resource
- Pew Internet Research (www.pewinternet.org) covers book-buying and reading habits as they relate to the internet. Search their topics for relevant research. They are also the best resource for social media use data.

It is worth noting here that book sales data can be controversial. The problem seems to be a lack of reporting standards. That may account for the variance in opinion of ebook sales, for instance.

You can also find genre-specific demographic information from professional groups. The Romance Writers of America provides data on who is reading romances, how often, and much more. If you write romance you can search their website for this information. Get in touch with the author groups associated with your genre and see if they provide data on book sales.

Social Media Data Galore

When it comes time to match readers of genre with users of social media, we are in luck. There is more free data on social media use out there than we really need. Thanks to websites like Pew Internet Research we have data on everyone's online behavior. And each of the major platforms such as Facebook, Twitter, Instagram, and Pinterest all have official blogs that provide platform-specific advice on their audiences.

Know Your Own People

Your best source of research is people who already read your books. You can use poll tools and promote a link to an informal research survey through your website, Twitter feed, Facebook page, or your email list. Doing a ten-question survey with your readers is free with a tool such as SurveyMonkey. You will be able to use SurveyMonkey's advanced analysis tools for free as well. I recommend doing a readership survey once a year. Use incentives to increase your responses such as offering a pool of prizes for random drawings from all the respondents. Or, you could offer a free download of a novella or other writing to each respondent. If you offer a free book for your newsletter signup, make sure it's a different one for your surveys. Gathering input from your dedicated readership is gold.

Below is an example of what your ten-question survey might look like with a tool like SurveyMonkey. You will notice I use a lot of ranked lists and multiple choice questions. You don't want people to input text for an answer, as the survey tool cannot analyze text. You will have to do that by hand. I also use the term Likert scale in this list. That is a list that allows people to rank an experience or opinion by a set criteria such as always, sometimes, hardly ever, and not at all.

What kinds of questions you ask depends on what you want to know about your audience. With only ten questions, you want to be focused on social media behavior and buying habits. First, start with general demographic questions so you can sort by them if you want to find out how each segment answers the questions in the survey as a group.

1. What is your age? Give them ranges to check. I suggest using the same age groups that Pew uses: 18-29, 30-49, 50-64, 65 and over. If you write for young adults you may want to add "under 18".

2. What are your favorite genres? Make this a multiple list they rank.

3. Do you have any favorite book review blogs you follow? The answer should be a text box. This is valuable research to find out where your readers get book recommendations. These answers can help you make decisions on where to advertise your books. SurveyMonkey will also turn these answers into a PDF for you that you can print or download.

4. What device or media do you like to read on? List the possibles (Kindle, Nook, iTunes, iPad, Kobo eReader, mobile phone, tablet, computer, print) make this a Lickert scale with four answers such as always, sometimes, hardly ever, not at all. A SurveyMonkey survey will put these together for you. Users can make one selection on each line. A single line might look like this:

Kindle: ____ **always** ____ **sometimes** _____ **not often** _____ **never**

5. Where do you buy your books? This would be similar to number four. List brick and mortar bookstores, Amazon, Barnes & Noble, Kobo, iTunes, author websites, social media, discount services like BookBub, Google Play, garage sales, and any other option you might be wondering about and use the same four or five Likert options.

6. What kind of information would you like to see in my newsletter? Have three options for your Likert scale on each: *like to see, neutral, don't care to see*. Items might include: new book announcements, contests, recommendations of good books by other authors, interactive polls, cover reveals, interviews with authors, pictures from hobbies or trips, interviews or reviews from readers, upcoming events, recipes, and whatever else you might want to know if they like. Have an "other" text box here as well. Your readers may have a stellar content idea you haven't considered.

7. What social media platforms do you use? This answer should be a Lickert scale with each platform on a separate line. Here's an example of what a line could look like:

1. Facebook: _ more than 5X/week _ 3-5X/week _ once a week _ not very often _ never

Use the same format for Twitter, Instagram, Pinterest, Tumblr, Snapchat, and Periscope. Add any channel you are currently using to reach your fans.

8. Do you do any of the following on social media or online? Again, a Likert scale of always, sometimes, hardly ever, not at all. This list should include: like a post, share a post, comment on a post, post a picture, tweet about a book you liked? Follow authors? Review a book on Goodreads? Review a book on Amazon? Participate in polls? Claim free offers? Buy a book directly from a social media ad or from a buy link posted by a friend or author?

9. What makes you want to buy a book? Have readers rank these choices: Friend recommendation, online reviews, cover, back cover blurb, email from an author I already read, discount or free, Amazon recommends, reviewed on a book blog I follow. Feel free to add your own suggestions.

10. What kind of information do you like to see on an author website? This question is similar to number six. List the kinds of features on a website and use a Likert scale to see how important they are. News of releases or latest books, contests, blog, contact information, bookshelf where I can purchase books, reviews of the author's books, personal information about the author, free offers or discounts, links to social media, check a backlist of older books, or whatever else you think is important.

Promote the survey for two weeks beginning in your newsletter, and then cross-promote it on social media and your website. After two weeks, the majority of people will ignore it. Remember that an incentive will help you get numbers. Once you have your numbers, you can analyze the data and use it to help you make marketing decisions. I recommend putting a disclaimer of sorts in your newsletter stating this is an annual event so they know you are not going to bombard them with a survey every month.

Who Are These People Anyway and What Difference Does It Make?

Analysis is often the hardest part of research. What do I do with all this data? Here are some observations that will help you pull feedback from the data to inform your marketing strategy.

1. Age: Do your readers match the norm for your genre? What age group has the biggest number? This will make a difference when you are choosing social media platforms and producing content.

2. **Favorite genres:** This gives you a good idea of which books your readers like and what other authors you can recommend.

3. **Favorite review blogs:** You can add these to your list of blogs to solicit reviews from. Also, sometimes these blogs offer inexpensive ads for cover features.

4. **Favorite device:** It might be that a decent percentage of your readers are on Kobo. Are you there yet? Make sure your books are available where your readers are.

5. **Buying habits:** This information helps you know where the calls-to-action should go when you promote your books.

6. **Newsletter suggestions:** Many authors struggle with content for newsletters. Now you can know what your readers would like to see.

7. **Social media information:** You can use this data for a couple things. First, cross-reference it with Pew data and see how it jives with the national norms. Pew has great data, but it's a starting point. What social media channels that your readers use are most important?

8. **Social media behavior:** You want to know more than what channels they use. What are they doing there? Are they seekers, amplifiers, or joiners? If they are just seeking information, you need to start thinking about content that will engage them take an action. You may have to ask them to share something important rather than take for granted that they will. We want to be moving people up the engagement ladder from seeking to amplifying to joining your community as a loyal fan.

9. **Buying motivations: what tips the sale for your readers?** Is it book covers? Then you better make sure yours are good. Is it a review from a friend? Maybe you need to develop a fan advocate program.

10. **Website information:** Every author needs a website. But it doesn't need to include everything. Find out what is most important for your readers.

After you analyze the information, you should have a pretty clear picture of who your readers are and the kinds of content and locations that will be most effective in reaching them. Other sources of audience research include comments on your Facebook page or Facebook group, blog comments, other authors' Facebook pages (in your genre), Pinterest likes and repins, retweets, and your email inbox. To really have a handle on your audience you have to listen to them, connect with them, and answer their questions. The more responsive you are, the better you will know them. The BookBub blog published a helpful article recently on how to identify your target audience here: http://bit.ly/1McSQgS.

Armed with some information on your readers, you can start to think about your marketing mix: what kind of content do they want?

Action Steps

1. Put together a short ten-question survey that you could send out to your email list subscribers and social media followers using the guidelines above. Brainstorm how the data you collect on each question would help you in your marketing.
2. Start an account on SurveyMonkey or a similar free surveying platform and put your survey together. Remember, make it 10 questions or less.
3. Publish the survey and send the link out to your followers. If you have a perma-free book, you may want to offer that as an incentive for taking the survey. Promote the link every other day on social media for ten days in addition to sending it out as an email blast.
4. If you decide to do numbers two and three, email me after you're done at chris@cksyme.com. I'd love to hear about your experience.

Chapter 9: Help Or Hype? To Sell Or Not To Sell

I got a chance to visit Disney World a couple of years ago during the International Food and Wine Festival. Our youngest daughter was running in a half marathon there and I was there for the food and wine. If you're a foodie and have been to this event, I can see you smiling right now. The festival is a smorgasbord that stretches around the entire circle in Epcot Center where countries sell their ethnic food and drink at kiosks to eager visitors. In addition, they have several food events, seminars, and pay-per special dinners you can go to. Since I enjoy the occasional cocktail, I thought it might be fun to go to a mixology class.

When we were seated, we found a placemat in front of us with three circles—one for each concoction that was going to be served. The mixologists each had several cookbooks (is that what you call a cocktail recipe book?) and proceeded to show how to make three wonderful potions, each with the utmost care and freshest ingredients. After each demonstration, we were all served a sample of the cocktail in a small glass gracefully placed in its circle on the placemat. It was a delicious experience.

One thing I learned about cocktails is that the mix or portion of alcohol is extremely important to the taste. We were taught that just like a food recipe, each ingredient is measured with care. Too much alcohol, and the drink can be turn the taste buds off.

The same is true in marketing. Building a loyal fan base is a matter of mixing the right portions of content that add value to content that sells. We have to find the proper mix of "helping to hype" to develop the kind of engagement that sells more books over the long haul. Constantly posting "please buy my book" is not helpful, it's annoying. People know you are going to sell occasionally. But you have to earn the right to sell, and when you do, you have a loyal customer on your hands.

How Can Our Marketing Content Create Loyalty?

According to Jay Baer, author of *Youtility*, helpful marketing content is the key to winning people's hearts, and in turn, their wallets.

"Youtility is marketing that's wanted by customers. Youtility is massively useful information, provided for free, that creates long-term trust and kinship between your company and your customers...You know that expression "If you give a man a fish, you feed him for a day; if you teach a man to fish, you feed him for a lifetime"? Well, the same is true for marketing: if you sell something, you make a customer today; if you help someone, you make a customer for life."

Baer says our paradigm shift starts with the understanding that we are not competing against other authors to sell our books, we are actually competing with our readers' friends for attention. We need to create friend-of-mine awareness. Baer writes:

"To succeed, your prospective customers must consider you a friend. And if, like their friends, you provide them real value, if you practice Youtility rather than simply offer a series of coupons and come-ons, they will reward you with loyalty and advocacy, the same ways we reward our friends."

What kind of content is useful? Marketo, an automation software company, conducts regular research about what is popular on social media. In their guide, *Contagious Content: What People Share On Facebook And Why They Share It*, they said the top shared Facebook posts fulfill one or more of the following functions:

- *Give*: Offers, discounts, deals or contests that everyone can benefit from, not just one sub-group of your fans.

- *Advise*: Tips, especially about problems that everyone encounters; for example, how to get a job or how to beat the flu.
- *Warn*: Warnings about dangers that could affect anyone.
- *Amuse*: Funny pictures and quotes, as long as they're not offensive to any group.
- *Inspire*: Inspirational quotes.
- *Amaze*: Amazing pictures or facts.
- *Unite*: A post that acts as a flag to carry and a way to brag to others about your membership in a group.

Combine that information with the types of content that are most popular (via Boom Social): pictures/images, opinions, recommendations and reviews, links to another website for information, news items, links to posts of others (shares, retweets, and pins), video clips, and plans for future activities such as travel.

We are trying to create an intersection between what our fans want and what we can deliver. The easiest way I know how to do that is using content buckets.

Your Bucket Lists

Content buckets help gather and organize social media content. It's user-friendly and not very time consuming. Each bucket represents the intersection between what your fans want and what you can provide for them. Each bucket is labeled with a content goal you have decided is valuable and helpful for your fans and doable for you. The content goals could be anything from entertainment to selling. There are three mandatory buckets that help us maintain that help-to-hype balance that is so important: Sales, Shout Outs, and Giveaways. The rest you choose based on what you like and what your customers need. Remember that the buckets represent a content type, not the specific media we use to deliver the content like images, video, text, links to news items, and so on. We'll talk about media later. The following is an example of what my content buckets might look like.

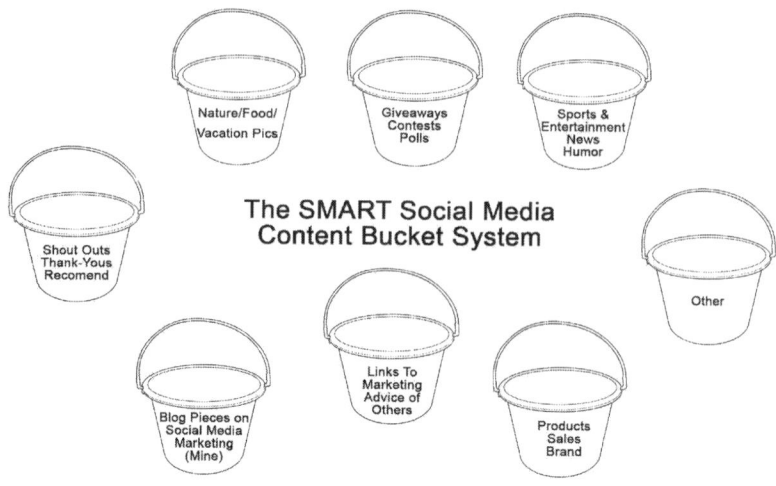

Mandatory Buckets

1. Products/Sales/Brand: This is the hype bucket. It's where I sell my books, promote my newsletter, classes, webinars, speaking engagements, and talk about my business services. This bucket is very tightly controlled because there is a certain amount of promotion I have to do on a regular basis. My followers know that I use social media to sell. I win their trust by giving way more than I take.

2. Shout Outs/Thank-Yous/Recommend: This is a necessary element for developing a spirit of generosity and a culture of reciprocity. Anyone who sells a product is indebted to their fans. Recommending other authors' books shows you are generous. Thinking that people only read your books is a scarcity mentality. Some authors shout out an occasional fan birthday, if they know it. Or thank someone periodically who is constantly sharing your online content. I have a client that sends handwritten thank-you notes with every prize she gives away in a promotion. Retweeting and sharing go in this bucket too.

3. Giveaways/Contests/Polls: Asking people what they think and then rewarding them for sharing is gold. I don't buy into the idea that too many promotions train your fans to always expect something for free. You have to be purposeful and interactive with your giveaways. It's okay to have them fill out a form occasionally to enter a giveaway. But when you run a promotion on a conversational platform like Facebook, make it about conversations and sharing. A weekly poll on a pop culture or entertainment news item is something your fans will enjoy participating in. People like to give their opinions. There are quite a few poll and quiz applications available including some apps that are connected directly to Facebook. Don't reinvent the wheel.

Personal Buckets

Besides mandatory buckets, I would pick some that express who I am as a person. I think fans can tell when you're passionate about something. I love travel, music, good eats, and I am a pretty rabid sports fan. Those are common human interests and connect me with my fans. I am also interested in establishing my expertise as a marketer so I have a blog with helpful information for my followers, and I also like to post articles by other marketers that I think my fans will find useful.

What are your interests? If you are an author, you are probably a reader. Think of common cultural and entertainment news items that you share with your fans. Have a sense of humor and have fun. Be yourself. How can you connect your books to this bucket? Do you have a large teen following? What are the issues important to them? Who are the entertainers they follow? Always think of finding common ground with your fans.

Filling the Buckets

I have a set of folders set up in Dropbox that are my "buckets." Whenever I see something online that looks like it might be a fit for a bucket, I dump it in the proper folder. You might like using Evernote or some other kind of content aggregator. I have folders for videos I find, inspirational quotes, images I take with my phone, links to articles I find, and anything else that strikes my fancy. However you organize your content is fine, as long as it is easily accessible and manageable. I pin a lot of this content to Pinterest private boards as well.

Your Buckets

I thought it might be fun to see what one of my client's content buckets look like. She is a romance and YA writer.

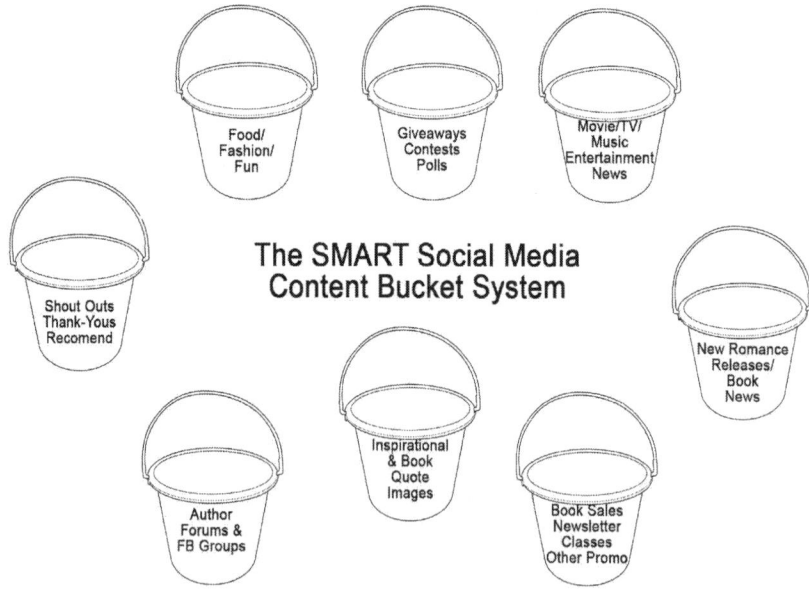

Help - I Am Not a Photographer!

Images and videos are very popular on the internet. The good news is you don't have to be a professional to take good pictures. And your phone camera is probably all you need. Here are a few tips for taking good photos for social media:

- **A picture is worth a thousand words.** Think of the story your images can tell. Make an emotional connection: a beautiful sunset or sunrise, a smiling baby, a good food picture, smiling or emotional faces (make sure and get close enough so fans can see the smiles).
- **Convey a sense of motion.** Are the subjects doing something? Are the trees bending with the wind? Waves washing on a beach? Somebody running or jumping?
- **Make sure the lighting is good.** If you are taking a picture against a lit background, like an open window, chances are the subjects will be very dark.
- **Make sure you know the right size for picture holes on each channel.** Keep a social media cheat sheet handy so you can crop pictures accordingly. Just Google "social media image cheat sheet" and you will find several.
- **Most picture holes are horizontal.** Plan accordingly—turn your phone sideways if you can.
- **For creative interest, use the rule of thirds:** divide your screen into thirds and place your subject in the right or left third.
- **Use a creative tool for adding text and effects.** There are a number of smartphone apps that do this. Canva is also a great place to import your photos and doctor them up.
- **Use high-resolution images.** There is nothing more amateurish than a pixelated photo. Don't enlarge a picture past its native size. The pixel size for good web photos is 72 dpi (dots per inch). However, if you blow up a 72 dpi image past its original size, it will get grainy quickly.

Simple images you can make with a tool like Canva or Photoshop:

- **Try your hand at memes.** Sometimes a picture you have taken would make a great meme.
- **Image quotes:** Readers like these creative adaptations of your books.
- **If you blog, make sure each article has an image.** If you can't find an appropriate one online, make a blog title image in Canva. They have a template for that. This is a must for Pinterest where you need an image to be able to pin your articles on a board.
- **Learn how to take screenshots.** A cropped screenshot can be a good image to share. Make sure whatever you are capturing is not copyright protected.

If you like to fiddle with video, more power to you. There is place for homemade video on social media, such as personal shout-outs or capturing an interview or special event. But if you are producing something for promotional purposes like a book trailer or a Periscope show, you should know your stuff. I recommend doing some research first: read up a book, take a course, or read how-to articles online. Badly produced video is abundant online.

Sometimes outsourcing video is not as expensive as you think. I can buy personalized video intros for my video webinars and classes for less than $10 each from IntroChamp. Just make sure you do your research if you are hiring someone. Check out their previous work and ask for recommendations if they don't have any video work posted on their website.

Next we'll take a look at how to use all those buckets to put together a content marketing mix.

Action Steps

1. Brainstorm what three of your personal content buckets might be. Make a list of what types of content you could put in those buckets.

2. If you are not a graphic artist, sign up for a free subscription to Canva and play around with it for a while. Subscribe to their Design School blog.

3. Bookmark a cheat sheet for social media images for easy reference so you know the sizes of images of different channels. Here is a good one from Visual.ly: http://visual.ly/social-media-image-size-cheat-sheet-2015

Chapter 10: The Marketing Mix

When my youngest daughter was a senior in high school, I took a group of high school volleyball players to Germany on a competitive tour. One of the other coaches had put together a list of German phrases she wanted us to get familiar with for the trip. I diligently learned them all plus a few more I thought were important. One day we stopped in a small town to grab some snacks at a grocery store. I wanted to use the restroom while I was there, so I approached one of the employees and asked (in German) where the bathroom was located. He began to gesture and give me detailed directions—in German.

After an embarrassing exchange trying to clarify that I didn't actually speak German, my daughter rescued me. She had several years of German in school and deciphered the directions for me. After a smiling thank-you, she reminded me not to ask a question in German unless I could understand the answer. My exchange with the young clerk was a failure because I broke a cultural rule: to communicate you have to speak the same language.

Social Media Is a Multicultural World

Now that you know which buckets make up your marketing mix, the next step is to get familiar with the unique culture of the various social media channels. In order to produce valuable content, you need to know how to apply cultural standards to your marketing mix. There are unwritten rules that will guide the perfect marketing mix.

So what does that perfect social media marketing mix look like? It depends on three factors: the maturity of your social media channels, whether your content is for a short-term or long-term campaign, and which social media channel you are using.

1. Social media maturity. This is a measurement of how long you have been developing your social media channels and how well that content engages your present fans. Mature here is not a measure of wisdom but a measure of age (like wine). If you have been on social media for a couple of years or more and your follower and engagement numbers have been consistently growing, then you are moving in the right direction. If you don't have a following on social media currently, you can't just jump in and start selling tomorrow. Nobody will follow you. You have to engage people first with content that interests them. You should already be a regular poster (according to the etiquette of the channel) and be actively drawing your followers in conversations. If not, you will need to make a correction and start building trust.

When you first start out on social media, your ratio of help to hype should be lopsided towards helping. You have to earn the right to sell, as Chris Brogan says. Brogan tells us this is simple, but not easy. Here are the steps he recommends to earn the right to sell on social media:

1. Define that circle you intend to serve. Who are they?
2. Learn their lore. What do they talk about and who are their heroes?
3. Shine your bat signal. Create great content that educates and informs.
4. Connect and share. Engage with the community that gathers.
5. Earn the right to sell and serve.

When you are building a community, you add value for a long time before you earn the right to sell. And you're not just promoting books. You are also building a platform by cross-promoting your social media channels on your website or posting a link to your newsletter signup on your Facebook page. There are subtle ways to promote. For instance, an image quote from your new book is an inspiring picture with a subtle sales twist. You have to find that sweet spot where people consider you a friend and not a salesperson.

Your fans know you want them to buy your books. Selling on social media requires the right mix. But unless it is secondary to adding value and making connections, people will avoid you.

2. Short- or long-term campaign. Believe it or not, there are times when you can tweak the normal marketing mix on social media. Short-term campaigns can qualify for an overload of posts in a short time. A short-term campaign has a defined beginning, a defined ending time, and a clear purpose. People know that the above average amount of posting and promoting are short lived. Here are some examples:

- Live events: If you are hosting or attending a live event such as a book signing, Facebook launch party, an awards party, or other noteworthy event, people will give you a pass on posting more than normal provided you are not using that volume to have private conversations you should be having via text message. If it is a real-time book party of some kind, let your fans know ahead of time (day before) that you will be posting frequently. Define the time period for them. Don't forget to invite them to the event if it is appropriate.
- Twitter chats and conference back channels: If you host a Twitter chat you should give your followers a heads up before it starts if you plan on participating or hosting. This can come in the form of a countdown tweet an hour out that reminds everyone that you will be starting at a certain time. If you attend a conference or workshop where there are social media hashtags and back channels for attendee discussions, let your followers know ahead that you will increasing your volume of posts. Again, invite them along if the content will be helpful for them.
- Book launch: If you use your social media channels to actively promote your book launch, be sure you don't inundate the exact same audience with email blasts for a week solid. Make a plan to integrate all your digital channels into a promotion schedule so you can see at a glance if you are being too disruptive.

Long-term campaigns are ongoing. They may be scheduled out a quarter or a year at a time, but they are the bedrock of your social media marketing plan. Here, you need to find the sweet spot of how many posts are good for your fans on all your channels. Building an email list is an example of a long-term campaign.

3. The channel. It is interesting to note that each social media channel out there has a culture. Just like society, each channel has developed unwritten rules of behavior. I've seen many creative "Social Media Explained" infographics over the years explaining the unique culture of every channel, and I thought you might enjoy this one using wine as the illustration from instamom101.com:

The purpose of the infographic is to illustrate how the audience, purpose, and context of conversations on each social media channel is different. What passes for good content on Facebook is not the same on Twitter. Let's take a closer look at some of the major channels. Just remember that the suggested posting practices are *long-term* practices and do not apply when you are running a *short-term* campaign.

Twitter: *I am drinking #wine:* Twitter is a real-time channel—it's all about what is going on right now. What is posted on Twitter quickly disappears in the sea of other tweets out there. Tweets are listed strictly in chronological order and avid Twitter users don't usually go back and peruse through their Twitter feeds once a day. There is just too much there. It's the newsroom. If something is happening now, people are following it on Twitter. Its 140 characters fuel a need to make tweets briefly engaging. Hashtags can also feed the fire by providing live clickable links to topics. Twitter is the CNN of the social media world.

Best posting practices: A good mix should involve 3-10 tweets per day spread out throughout the major drive times (morning, afternoon, evening). Yes, you need to schedule or time your tweets to hit every audience in real time. Whatever you do, don't shove them out all at once.

Remember your global audience if you market your books to other parts of world. For instance, the United Kingdom is a good market for me so I keep a note on my computer reminding me of the ideal times to tweet in London. I schedule those tweets with SproutSocial as I am not usually up at two in the morning.

Facebook: *I like wine*. Facebook has built an empire being the place where people get together to share, post pictures, and upload video about what they like. It is the living room, the backyard fence. It is by far the best developed and most popular social media channel on the internet. According to Pew Internet's annual report, 71 percent of the adults online in the U.S. are on Facebook. It becomes an even bigger deal when you see that the next nearest channel is a tie between LinkedIn and Pinterest at 28 percent. Numbers don't tell the whole story of any social media channel, but you cannot ignore Facebook's numbers.

Best posting practices: It's important to develop an active community on your Facebook page because their algorithm will punish you if you are not. The algorithm is a formula Facebook uses to decide which posts are the most popular with users. It is a multiplier that allows more of your fans to see a post as its popularity increases. The more people who interact with your posts, past and present, the more people will see them. If you have a business Facebook page, each post is accompanied by data under the post that tells you exactly how many people your post reached. You calculate your engagement based on how many people interacted with it compared to how many fans of your fans it could reach. If you have 750 fans and your post only reached 15 of them, then that piece of content was not particularly engaging. It didn't get enough traction to reach more people because your content wasn't good enough for people to interact, for whatever reason. But as I will show you later in the book, more isn't better on Facebook. Better is better. Facebook forces you to post good content. A beginning guide for posting frequency is two or three times per day spread out during the day.

Instagram: *Here is a vintage photo of my favorite wine.* Instagram boasts 26 percent of the general online adult population according to Pew, but 53 percent of their audience is in the 18-29 age bracket. Instagram is all about pictures that tell a story. It is possible to upload graphics to Instagram, but it is a storytelling platform not really known for being a conversation platform like Facebook. You can like pictures of people you follow and comment on people's pictures. But interaction on Instagram is not about people, it's about the pictures. Hashtags on Instagram are good for real-time events and following conversations. Instagram is your online picture gallery.

Best posting practices: Frequency on Instagram isn't as important as remembering not to batch upload there (posting a large group of pictures at once). Keep in mind that your pictures run through your followers' news feeds, and the last thing they want is a string of 15 photos in a row of your book signing. Load large groups of photos into a Facebook album instead and let your followers on Instagram know they can find more on your Facebook page in your comment.

YouTube: *Watch me drink wine.* Even though Facebook is giving YouTube a run for its money with video, you can't beat YouTube's search advantage (owned by Google). It is the second largest search engine on the internet. At this writing, it is still the best channel on the internet for marketing with video. Vimeo is a good competitor, especially for long-form video but does not have the search capabilities of YouTube.

Best posting practices: Since YouTube is a personal production channel in that you actually have to produce a video and upload it, make sure that your videos are valuable. This might be a good channel to use if you are thinking of posting a regular news or entertainment feature, or you have high quality book trailers. Notice the emphasis on "high quality".

Pinterest: *Here's a recipe for cooking with wine.* Although Pinterest is a valuable place to get recipes, it is also a place to buy anything and everything from individuals or even stores like Nordstrom. Pinterest is quickly becoming a major channel for retail. They have announced several upgrades coming in the next year to make Pinterest more of a commerce channel including direct buy buttons.

Pinterest is not just for women anymore, but they are still the biggest demographic: 42 percent of women online use Pinterest compared to 13 percent of online men. Pinterest is not, at this time, a platform where discussions take place but re-pins (sharing the posts of others) are the currency of engagement on Pinterest. Pin boards can cover any subject matter which makes it the perfect blank canvas for diverse subject matter. Many people mix business and their personal life on Pinterest. It's a good way to give fans a little peek into your life.

Best posting practices: Buffer claims that you should post five times a day on Pinterest. I don't think that is necessary unless you are a major brand with loads of content to share. I think the more important key on Pinterest for authors is to have boards that are interesting to your fans and keep them current. I would suggest maintaining a regular posting time on Pinterest rather than a number of posts. Since repinning is a major fan booster on Pinterest, you need to consider a Pinterest strategy that revolves around following as well as posting. Some authors have a board for every book, some have recommendation boards for other authors in their genre. You can also invite fans to pin on specific boards. This can be especially fun in a contest.

Tumblr: *I blog about wine.* Tumblr is a free blogging platform that has a younger demographic—their biggest age group is 18 to 24. Because of that skew, Tumblr is becoming a popular site for teen reviewers of young adult books. Publishers gearing to teens are also there. See this list of the 28 Must Follow Tumblrs For Fans Of YA from Book Riot (http://bookriot.com/2014/08/16/tumblr-ya-fans/). Young adult authors are also recruiting influential reviewers on Tumblr. The numbers on Tumblr drop significantly over age 45.

Best posting practices: Since Tumblr is a blogging platform, you should be posting at least once a week or you will not be able to compete with all the noise out there. A couple times a week would be ideal. Tumblr readers also like shorter content so you don't have to post long-form content there. Images with captions or motivational quotes with a line or two on why it is motivational to you are perfectly acceptable on Tumblr. Also, it's important to know the audience here. I would suggesting following some bloggers in your genre before you jump in.

A Word About the Rest

I did not mention anything about LinkedIn, Spotify, Foursquare, Vine, Snapchat, or Google Plus because I do not consider those channels primary for authors (LinkedIn would be an exception for non-fiction writers). That doesn't mean you won't find an audience on those channels. I just think that the amount of time you have to spend being engaging on those channels won't give you a proportional return unless you work really hard at it. They don't fit the SMART paradigm of manageable for most authors. If you have a lot of time on your hands and want to try experimenting with Snapchat or Vine, go for it. For most authors, even those who have younger readers, they are a waste of time. We'll talk more about the why later.

Action Steps

1. Which social media channels do you think are a good fit for your audience and why?
2. Does your schedule have room at this time for you to do some research on the channels you mentioned above? If not, is it worth reworking your time to add them now?
3. Given the information in this chapter, are there any social media channels you are currently on that you should rethink?

Chapter 11: Brand Advocates - How To Build Raving Fans

Pop quiz! You are a contemporary romance writer. You want to build a following of *loyal* fans. What would you rather have: one tweet from Scarlett Johansson mentioning one of your novels or 200 engaged followers in an exclusive Facebook group? The best answer for building loyal fans is the latter. Scarlett Johansson can give you an immediate sales boost today, but that influence is gone tomorrow. You can retweet it only so many times before your fans think you are cheesy. Yes, put it in your Amazon book description, but that only works for this book. She is an influencer, in marketing terms, not an advocate. And if you are looking to develop a loyal following, you want advocates. If you're looking for a short-term spurt, influencers are a good bet. Just for the record, I'd like both.

Influencers Vs. Advocates

Understanding influencers and advocates is a SMART social media marketing fundamental because both audiences possess the ability to amplify your social media signals with different results. One is temporary (influencers) and one is long-term (advocates). Authors need advocates to build a loyal following of raving fans, but influencers can create a viral burst of energy that can temporarily boost sales or bring attention to your brand.

Influencer marketing is popular at the writing of this book. Agencies are even springing up as handlers for stars with huge social media followings on micro content channels like YouTube, Vine, Snapchat, and Instagram. The social media company *Visual.ly* defines micro content as short-form content optimized for social media and designed to combat information overload. Jay Baer calls it snackable content. Its main defining element is length, whether written or visual. Instagram has a video time limit of 15 seconds,

Vine has a cap at six seconds, and Snapchat stories disappear in 24 hours.

Snapchat phenom Shaun McBride ("Shonduras" on Snapchat) commands top dollar renting out his audience for Disney, Taco Bell, Major League Soccer and other national brands. Authors of teen books are seeking out YouTube book reviewers with large young adult audiences to help promote their books. It's a form of celebrity endorsement, as brands seek influencers in their target audience with large audiences for short-term campaigns.

Influencer marketing relies on two things: a talented social media star who can produce engaging content and a huge following. But there are a couple of problems. The influencer's audience is just rented and the audience will more likely follow the influencer to the next destination and forget about you. Even though influencer marketing has its advantages it lacks the trust factor that people often need to make a purchase based on the recommendations of others. Many people see these celebrity endorsements as just paid advertising.

What Is a Brand Advocate?

According to Rob Fugetta's book, *Brand Advocates*, "brand advocates are highly-satisfied customers and others who proactively recommend brands and products online and offline without being paid to do so." They are your dedicated readers. Taking that one step further, they are people who recommend your stuff to others. They can be found through a newsletter, a Facebook page, an event, or even through personal contact. In Fugetta's book, he stresses the importance of understanding that brand advocates don't recommend you for the rewards, they recommend you because they like to help other people.

What's The Difference Between Influencers and Advocates?

The difference between an influencer and an advocate is well illustrated in the infographic below, a joint venture between Zuberance and Convince and Convert. There are two key differences between advocates and influencers that affect purchases: level of consumer trust and advocacy and loyalty. Advocates are long-haul people. They love your brand, they love your products. They consider you a personal purveyor of value. That is why there is such a higher trust level with their reviews and social media posts. They deliver the why to your potential readers. Influencers give you a lot of eyeballs (reach), but their influence on rate of conversion and return purchases is lower because a fan's connection is to the influencer, not to the brand.

INFLUENCERS | BRAND ADVOCATES

Consumer Trust

18% Trust Influencers
(source: Forrester Research Inc.)

92% Trust Brand Advocates
(source: Nielsen)

Typical Profile

Pundit
Blogger
Celebrity

Highly-Satisfied Customer

Defined By

(Twitter followers, blog subscribers, etc.)

Size of Audience

How likely they are to recommend the brand

Motivation

Grow Audience

Help Friends
(source: comScore)

Also see this informative piece by Jay Baer for more information on why advocates are superior to influencers: http://bit.ly/1N5GGMs. In this article, Baer fine-tunes the differences:

"We tend to confuse audience with influence. Having a large Twitter or blog following doesn't inherently make a person influential. It gives them an audience, and very few influencers have enough juice to drive action in droves.

Brand advocates are a sustainable marketing force. Advocates crave engagement from your brand. Unlike influencers, they are eager to support, promote, and defend your brand on a long-term basis. Plus, their trusted recommendations affect each part of the purchase funnel driving substantial business results."

Fan Groups: How to Find and Nurture Advocates

Fan groups are the best place to build dedicated advocates. I've found that there are two very effective ways to find and build brand advocates in different sectors, but the two I've had the most success with across the board are Facebook groups and newsletter segments. For nonfiction authors who also teach online courses or host webinars, newsletter segments associated with those products are very effective. I would like to expand on Facebook group pages here.

A Facebook group is not a business page. It is a special category of Facebook pages designed to foster discussions and more personal relationships. Business pages are easily searched on Facebook and the internet, but groups are a little harder to find. However, the discovery piece (finding you on the internet) is not a goal of a Facebook fan group. The goal is to bring together people who already know and love your books. Facebook groups have some dynamic attributes you can take advantage of:

1. **They can be private or public.** Private groups require an administrator to grant a request to be included in the group. If the purpose of your group is just to have a discussion around a cause, public might be a better option. If you want to develop a group of brand advocates, keep the group private. This creates a great "insider" feel and keeps the spam out.

2. **Sharing stays within the group.** Members can interact with one another, but cannot share posts from the group outside the group unless it is a public group. Again, it's all about the insider feel. But remember, advocates see themselves as helpers of people. They want access to insider info, but they want to share the good news to get other people inside. Encourage them to use their own social media channels to bring in new group members.

3. **As of this writing, group posts still appear in the news feed and as a notification.** There is no engagement algorithm in place with Facebook groups that constrains the number of posts people see. Everyone in the group is notified when the group admin posts and admin posts will run in the news feed automatically unless users change their individual settings. To me, this is a key aspect of a

group. My little "world" of notifications on the Facebook page header keeps me on top of the people and posts that are most important to me regardless of what Facebook's algorithm says. Facebook groups currently have an advantage when it comes to promoting engagement.

4. You can create special group events. Groups have the same event functions that regular pages do. You can do contests, giveaways, and have chats.

5. A group can be a place where you reach out personally to your fans. This is much easier to do in a controlled Facebook group than on a business page. You should be responding to fans on your author business page as well, but the conversations you start in your group are more intimate as the group feels more like a community.

6. Groups are another level of engagement in, so to speak, so they need more tending. If you start a group, you will need to be active there. Fans come into a group to connect with you. Be there.

Plan to Succeed

Starting a fan group and cross-promoting it requires some planning. It would be wise to sit down and answer the following:

- What are the benefits of being in my Facebook group? What value will it add to members?
- How can I give them the tools to be true brand advocates? What kind of content will I need?
- What goals do I have for this group?
- Do I have time to manage a small private group in addition to all my other duties?
- What are the benefits to my brand of starting a fan group? How am I going to thank them?
- Do I want to set any rules for my group such as no spamming or no promoting personal products and services?
- What promotional channels can I use to build the group?

Having a core group of advocates for your brand has many benefits:
- They can be a springboard to develop an advance reader team or a social media ambassador team that will provide honest reviews of your products or help amplify your social media messages.
- They can use word of mouth to help you find new fans among their friends.
- They can be a source of social media content (commonly called user-generated content).
- They can provide recommendation snippets for your website and advertising.
- They can be a source of research when you want to know what fans think.

Just remember that your advocates like rewards and exclusive offers as well as the rest of us. The big difference is that rewards are not necessarily their motivation for being a brand advocate. They just want to help connect you with other people.

Action Steps

1. If you have a Facebook page, go through the last four weeks of posts and take note of people who have interacted with your posts on a regular basis. Start a document or database and keep track of your loyal followers. Make note of what kinds of actions they are taking. A share is a more important action than a like. Do the same for any other main social media channels you have.

2. Brainstorm what kind of content you could produce that is exclusive for this group. Do you like or favorite or retweet their posts as a thank-you occasionally?

Part III - The SMART Social Media Marketing Toolbox

The tool department in any hardware store can be overwhelming, especially when you have an important project and you want it done right. It's easy to fall into the trap of thinking that more tools will give you a better outcome, but you may end up with tools you don't need. If I wanted to build a doghouse, I would not go in and buy one of everything in the store to make sure I have all my bases covered. I would buy only the tools I truly need to do the job. But to accomplish that, I would need a plan and a shopping list.

The selection of tools for social media is just as overwhelming. There are too many choices and they seem to change daily, so in this next section I'll provide a map of what to use and why. Let's start with some tool talk.

Chapter 12: Too Many Tools To Choose From (Or How To Avoid Shiny Object Syndrome)

There are over 200 social media networking sites listed on Wikipedia along with the disclaimer that it is not an exhaustive list. How did this space get so crowded? Let's look at the history of social media in a nutshell.

- 1991: The worldwide web is invented by British computer scientist Sir Tim Berners-Lee.
- 1994: The first web blog was penned by Swarthmore college student Justin Hall, even though the term "blog" didn't come along until around 1999.
- 1999: Blogger emerges as the first readily available online blogging platform launched by Pyra Labs. Today, it belongs to Google (as does most everything else).
- 2000: Wikipedia is launched.
- 2002: Friendster launches as the first social network site. It was remade into a gaming site in 2011.
- 2002: LinkedIn is conceived by Stanford graduate Reid Hoffman. As of this writing, it is the leading site for networking in the business sector.
- 2003: MySpace is born.
- 2004: Facebook comes on the scene. It reaches one billion users in 2012.
- 2005: YouTube launches a free social video sharing site.
- 2006: Twitter emerges.
- 2010: Instagram is released. By December 2014, it has over 300 million active users.
- 2011: Google Plus is launched.
- 2011: Pinterest is launched and becomes the third largest social network by March 2012.
- 2011: Snapchat initial release. By August 2014, the platform boasts over 100 million users.

- 2012: Pew Internet Research reports that 45 percent of adults own a smartphone. Edison Research reports that more than half of Facebook users access the site via mobile phone.
- May 2013: WebX reports that 60 percent of U.S. adults are not aware of Facebook privacy settings.
- June 2013: Pew Internet issues research saying that the majority of Americans own smartphones and access the internet with those devices.
- Summer 2014: Yik Yak, an anonymous location-based messaging app linked to bullying, causes a stir taking their mascot on an aggressive promotional tour of college campuses across the U.S. to elevate its reputation as a mainstream application for students.
- March 2015: Pew Internet research reports 92 percent of American teens go online daily, including 24 percent who go online "almost constantly".
- Summer 2015: Periscope takes off as a Twitter-based live streaming option for mobile phones.

The Superhighway of Social Media

It is amazing to look at the above list and see that the most popular social media tools are less 15 years old. And more tools hit the internet daily. Some fizzle quickly, and others get traction and claim a little piece of the pie. Little indeed—that pie is not evenly divided.

According to Pew Internet data from 2014, a whopping 71 percent of adults online in the U.S. are on Facebook. But the nearest competitors —Twitter, LinkedIn, Pinterest, and Instagram—hover around 25 percent. The 13- to 17-year-old population looks a little different. Their top platforms are Facebook (71%), Instagram (52%), Snapchat (41%), Twitter and Google Plus (33%), Vine (24%) and Tumblr (11%).

There are more than 30 billion pieces of content shared on Facebook every month. According to Twitter, there are 500 million tweets posted every day. An average of 70 million images are shared on Instagram daily. Add websites and email to that list and you have a flood of information flowing on the internet that is impossible to keep up with. Everyday we are inundated with more messages than we can absorb. How do you decide what social media channels will help you break through the traffic to reach potential readers and sell more books?

Start by Asking SMART Questions

When deciding which tools to take out of the toolbox, start with five SMART questions:

1. Can this tool be part of a sustainable marketing plan?

Some social media tools are built with a very narrow focus. Tools like Snapchat and LinkedIn address niche markets. In order to embrace either of those channels for marketing, their audience should match your target audience. If they do not, they will not create much traction for you. But that's not the only requirement.

Snapchat, in addition to appealing to a young audience, is limited to real-time content that disappears in 24 hours with no archive ability. It is a messaging platform that needs constant attention. Successful brands on Snapchat produce engaging story-based content on a regular basis. If you write for young adults, have some time on your hands, can put together a creative storyboard, and are good with your phone camera, then you might want to give it a shot. Just remember that your ability to attract new readers is extremely low on Snapchat. People need an exact username to search someone on Snapchat. Consequently, it requires cross-promotion on other social media channels to point potential users to your account.

Sustainability is also about risk/reward for the long run. Some channels like Facebook deliver rewards with minimal risk because of the channel's sheer numbers and diverse audience. But channels with narrower audiences are higher risk because they require you to hit a smaller sweet spot with your content. That doesn't mean you shouldn't consider them. That just means they shouldn't be the primary channel in your social media plan if your reader audience is not prominent there.

2. If I add this tool to my social media marketing plan, will it be manageable?

All tools are not created equal. Some have a higher learning curve than others. Some require more time to produce content. Some demand higher posting frequencies and require more attention. Some tools require purchasing equipment or subscriptions. Tools can be a strain on time, money, and resources. Before you add a tool to your marketing mix, you have to count the cost.

- *Assess how you use your time*: I'll bet your day is full. But do you know what it's filled with? Before you can add something, you have to take something away or consolidate some tasks. Keep a diary for a week detailing how you use your time. If you are spending an hour every day scouring Facebook for personal use, that is probably a waste of your time. How many hours do you watch TV? Could you get by on two instead of three? Can you get up a half hour earlier everyday? I highly recommend reading Joanna Penn's *How To Make A Living With Your Writing*. Her book will walk you through an author-specific process of making the best use of your time. Talk to author friends and see how they manage their time. This is an important discussion.
- *Assess your budget*: Writing involves prioritizing expenses. There are mandatory costs like book covers and editing. Spending money on marketing is not a top level expense for most. But there are marketing assets you should invest in to step up your books sales and reach new readers such as a website and an email service.
- *Assess what resources you need to make social media marketing manageable*: What is your current level of social media

marketing expertise? Would you consider yourself a beginner? How much of your marketing can you do? What will you need to hire out? Are you going to need training to be able to manage your own marketing? Do you have a source where you can find the help you need? If not, check Chapter 20 for some help.

3. Is this tool a good match for my audience?

If we take the information in Chapter 4 (Audience-Specific) and add the information from Chapter 10 (The Marketing Mix), we have everything we need to answer this question.

4. Is this tool relevant to my marketing goals?

In Chapter 5 we learned that relevance is about matching specific content to a specific audience. Snapchat is a good example of a platform whose relevance is strongest with people under 25 years of age. As an author, you have to decide if the Snapchat audience base is a match for your reader audience base. If not, don't waste your time.

5. Does this tool match a goal or strategy that I have already defined in my marketing plan?

Don't let tools distract you from your goals. Evaluate your motivations. If it's a new platform, how will it fit into your strategy or are you just drawn to the tactic? Is "fear of missing out" motivating you? Can you afford to wait a while and see how the tool develops? Don't let Shiny Object Syndrome lead you down a path where you are a jack of all trades and master of none.

Action Steps

1. Are you spreading yourself too thin by trying to be present on too many social media channels? Make a plan to evaluate the effectiveness of all your platforms to make sure they are helping you reach your goals and reaching your specific audience.
2. What new social media platforms have you seen that interest you? Find someone to follow on those platforms and see what kind

of content they are producing. How much work would it take for you to have the same success? What will the learning curve be? The cost?

Chapter 13: The Big Three -Websites, Mailing Lists, And Facebook…Oh My

One of my favorite restaurants in Las Vegas is Le Village Buffet in the Paris Hotel. Le Village is a sophisticated departure from your average Vegas buffet, and breakfast is their crown jewel. On each visit, my husband and I approach the buffet with differing strategies. I like to wander and randomly sample a little of everything until I am stuffed. He, on the other hand, chooses a few of the classics and puts together a more traditional breakfast. He has a plan that fits his stomach; I do not.

Some people think of social media as a smorgasbord of delights. A little of this and a little of that until we are stuffed to the gills. But this strategy is not compatible with our SMART framework. To succeed we must establish priorities when we step up to the buffet.

In the next three chapters I will develop these priorities in layers: The Big Three, The Next Three, and The Playground. We'll start with the Big Three. These are the non-negotiable necessities of book marketing. To start on the path to successful book marketing, you need a website, a Facebook Page, and an email list.

1. Your Website Is the Hub

Yes, your website is a social media channel. Not in the traditional sense, but it is in today's marketing environment. Here are three factors driving this truth:
- Google hosts about 3.5 billion searches a day as of this writing and Facebook processes around 1.5 billion searches. According to Alexa, the keeper of all internet stats, the top three websites in the world are Google, Facebook, and YouTube.

- Social media profiles routinely show up on the first page of Google search results making your social media profiles main portals of discovery.
- Websites are now considered part of the viral marketing loop of "inbound marketing," a method of attracting fans with keywords, blogs, and social media content that focuses on pulling people toward your brand or product. This contrasts with old school outbound marketing methods of buying ads, billboards, and direct mail that send your product out to people in hopes you are hitting the right people at the right time and the right place. Inbound marketing is considered "opt-in" content. Outbound marketing is considered interruptive.

The Downside of Social Sharing on Websites

A couple years ago, negative information about the mix of websites and social sharing made the rounds on website development sites. Stats were showing that people were seeing social media icons on a website header and leaving to visit the company's social media before spending any time on the website. Today, social networking is evolving to mirror web content by branding and content, evolving into a website partner rather than a detractor.

Today, almost any " website function" such as capturing leads, email newsletter sign-ups, and selling products is also done on social media. Pinterest is a virtual mall. Twitter cards can do everything from capture leads to sell products. Facebook has "Buy Now" buttons and ecommerce capabilities. The argument that social media detracts from your website is no longer valid—the two work hand in hand.

Why You Need a Website

Until the internet evolves into a place where search is not important, you will need a website to be found. You can be found on Amazon or iTunes, but you need real estate you control.

Also, lack of a website looks unprofessional. How do you feel about a business when you do an online search and find they don't have a website? You can set up a basic website for free on WordPress so there is no excuse for not having one. A custom domain that increases your search potential may cost you $20. Your website can host a bookstore (with links to Amazon and other sales venues), a blog, your bio, your email newsletter sign-up, links to your social media channels, and it gives readers a sense of who you are at a glance. Your website is like your book cover. It influences a reader's first impression and makes them want to turn the page. Make it a good one.

Where to Start

WordPress is the go-to platform for user-friendly websites. WordPress.com hosts websites for free and there are some easy add-ons available, like a custom domain, for a small annual fee. If you don't buy a custom domain your website will be harder to search as its address will be www.wordpress.com/yournamehere. With a custom domain, you have a dedicated searchable address. WordPress.org is the place where you buy a "theme" or template that is hosted online by a service such as GoDaddy, Bluehost, and others. This option is more expensive but you should be able to get a basic website put together for less than $200. The WordPress management system for posting new content, ads, and other information is user-friendly and there are hordes of how-to videos available on YouTube and from WordPress experts online. There are other website companies out there, but I recommend WordPress. They have the best integration with email systems and free plugins to enhance your website. WordPress will also grow with you, especially if you are considering selling your own books directly to readers at some point.

Avoid using Google's Blogger as a website venue. Their platform has very few design or integration options. I think it is an indicator that your blog is older and you haven't made an effort to update or refresh your look. You can use custom domains with Blogger but the platform is set up for blogging and doesn't have the flexibility or add-ons that WordPress has.

Because of the interactive nature of websites today you need to keep your website populated with fresh content. This assures that visitors won't see the same old stuff and the Google bots that visit won't think you're dead. I suggest undertaking some training if you want to manage your own website. Also, follow a blogger or two that knows website marketing for regular tips and news. Network with fellow authors and ask for their opinions and insights.

2. Email Addresses Are Your Golden Link to Fans

Books have been written and courses taught on how to build an email subscription list. Why the hoopla? Because email addresses are the highest level of fan opt-in you can get. Subscribers give up their personal emails to receive something they deem valuable from you. In his book *Platform*, Michael Hyatt gives these seven strategies for building an email list:
- Generate content worth reading.
- Use a dedicated list subscription system like MailChimp or AWeber.
- Make your sign-up form highly visible on all your main internet channels.
- Offer an incentive for subscribing.

- Design a branded email template to use when you send an email that fans will recognize.
- Follow up with your subscriber with a welcoming email.
- Use common locations to promote your sign-up form such as social media bios, Facebook apps, and blog article footers.

Today, author marketing experts like Mark Dawson and others are advocating that authors put an email list opt-in in the front and back matter of all their ebooks. Motivate sign-ups with a "perma-free" book, novella, or prequel to a series. Dawson also advocates advertising on Facebook and other platforms to grow your lists. In his free video course he lets viewers know what a sales advantage it is to have a large email list when it's time to launch a new book.

Word of Caution

The inbox is a sacred place for many people. If fans give you permission to email them, make every email count. Don't spam people or sell their emails to others. And don't buy email lists from others. This could get you banned from some email providers. Make sure you are offering good free content on a regular basis through your email list. These people are your most valued fans, so give them first class treatment. Don't be afraid to tell them how to unsubscribe. Better that than having them file a complaint with the email provider. If you're providing good content, they'll stick with you.

There is a wealth of email newsletter training courses out there including several from email providers themselves. I use AWeber and it has an extensive help section. Take some time to educate yourself about effective email marketing so you don't lose an email address as quickly as you get it. Learn how to use this precious resource carefully.

3. Facebook Is the King of Social Media

Facebook is the only true social media network that I recommend for every author. And the reason is based on numbers and audience. Let's look at the facts first:
- According to Pew Internet Research, 71% of online American adults (age 18+) use Facebook. It has the most even distribution across gender, age, and ethnic groups of any other social media channel. Facebook does the best job of delivering relevant information and services to their users.
- Facebook makes more money from ad revenue than all other channels put together.
- The next four most popular channels only reach 28% or less of online adults.

All this glowing data needs to be tempered with some reality. Even though Facebook is king, there are some question marks to consider:
- Social Media Examiner's Annual Marketing Report indicates that half of marketers don't know whether their social media marketing is effective. This may be due to the fact that marketers find some of social media's key benefits, such as developing loyal fans, difficult to measure.
- Facebook's *engagement algorithm* (a formula they use to decide what your fans will see) rewards content that people like and share. If you have 500 fans but your posts are only seen by 20 people, Facebook will be a tough nut to crack for you. It is this agonizing algorithm that is responsible for the wealth of Facebook marketing advice online. You can't game the algorithm but you can beat it. Just post good content. Keep track of what works and what doesn't. Stay on top of Facebook. No other social media channel at present changes their "rules of engagement" as often as Facebook does.

Note: When you see articles from people who claim to have "hacked" the Facebook algorithm, don't buy it. What we need to pay attention to is good advice on how to increase the engagement of our posts because that is what the algorithm rewards.

So are we damned if we do and damned if we don't? Not quite. The trick is to understand how to use Facebook correctly. When you do, it can return valuable rewards. But it does take work. I wouldn't stay up nights trying to figure out how to conquer Facebook, but I would make sure I stayed educated on best practices there. You can follow a couple of people online to get all the latest Facebook information: Mari Smith and Jon Loomer. Mari Smith has an excellent Facebook page filled with helpful tips. I recommend Loomer for people who are already using Facebook for marketing and need more advanced advice.

Before you dive into the next section, you need to get a general understanding about the different types of Facebook pages: personal profile, Facebook Pages, and Facebook Groups. This link from Mashable (http://mashable.com/2014/10/19/facebook-pages-groups-profiles/) will get us started. Here are a few key observations from the article:

- **Personal profile:** A Facebook profile is a page you set up for your personal use. You set the privacy levels and approve every friend request individually. There are limited opportunities here to use Facebook ads and no audience data is available. Facebook asks that people do not use personal profiles for commercial use.
- **Facebook Page:** A Page or business page is designed for promotion of an individual or a brand. With a Page, you have access to the full stable of Facebook ads, access to audience and engagement data in their Insights dashboard and can choose from a wide variety of apps to enhance your page. Anyone can like your page—you don't approve followers. However, you can set privacy levels on who can post on your page and who can see what.
- **Facebook Group:** Groups are a way for people to gather around a cause or brand. They are similar to forums. Groups can be public, private (have to be added by an administrator) or secret (open to anyone but have to be added by a member).

The biggest problem we all have is identifying the differences between a personal profile and a Page. If it is still fuzzy, stop here, go back and read the Mashable article again and the bullet points above. This understanding is critical in knowing how to use Facebook to market.

Making the Most of Facebook

There are two main ways authors can use Facebook for their business. The first is setting up an official fan Page where fans follow you by liking your Page. The second is to set up a private Facebook Group for devoted fans. I recommend authors consider both, but at a minimum, set up an official Page.

Facebook Groups can offer a number of opportunities that pages do not afford. By opting in, group members step up to a new level of loyalty whereas people on an official Page will have different levels of advocacy from people who have never read one of your books to avid readers. I recommend that you take some time to read this article I wrote on how to develop raving fans with a Facebook group here: bit.ly/1LXdE03. It will help you understand the nuts and bolts of building a successful group and why you should consider it.

Think of your official fan Page as a department store that offers something for everyone. You can create events for your book launches, ask weekly questions to spur discussions, or post beautiful image quotes from your new book and post links to entertaining videos you find. In addition, you gather information there such as email addresses. You can also actively sell your books there. It is a directory of sorts as well with links to your other social media outposts and your website.

Think of your Facebook Group as a private party where you need an invitation to get in but everybody is invited. Groups house fans who want a deeper experience than your official fan Page. To give the group an insider feel and keep it aimed at developing advocacy, I recommend making your group closed so members have to be admitted by an administrator. I will go into depth about how to set up a Facebook Group in the book's bonus materials so be sure and sign up to receive them in the back of the book.

Since this group expects a deeper experience than they get on your page, make it worth their while. Offer exclusive giveaways, regular discussions, and give them sneak peeks of things like book covers. Many authors have developed robust advance reader teams through Facebook Groups in addition to crowdsourcing character names, covers, plot ideas, and other elements of their books. If you are energized by connecting with people, a Facebook Group might be a good option for you. Nonfiction writers can develop successful Groups also.

A big advantage of a Facebook group is that members receive a default notification when an administrator posts and, as of this writing, posts from group administrators automatically appear in their news feed. This function bypasses the powerful algorithm that restricts what people see normally in their news feeds—something you don't get on regular Facebook Pages. Facebook considers Groups a high opt-in experience and pushes post notifications out to everyone unless they have set their settings to exclude group notifications. You may need to pay more attention to the traffic in your Group because of your fans' expectations.

One disadvantage of a private group is that posts cannot be shared outside the group. I know one author who gets around this by providing pre-written posts and images for members to cut and paste on to their personal Facebook pages during giveaways and book launches to get new members into the group.

Before you get flustered about creating content for two separate Facebook pages remember that the Facebook Group members will ultimately drive a lot of the content and interaction. They join the group with the expectation of joining a family. Family members interact more freely than fans on a Facebook page. Many authors use Facebook groups as a sort of insider's club for their fans.

Word of Caution

I do not recommend you use your personal profile as a platform for your author brand. I have worked with authors who tried to do this and it turned out poorly. Besides the fact that it is a hassle to have to accept every fan as a friend, you will not have some of the Facebook business benefits such as Insights (data about your users) or access to some advertising opportunities. Keep your business life separate and protect your private family life. Facebook states that "Personal profiles are for non-commercial use."

If you have already started using your personal profile as an official page and don't want to lose your followers, Facebook has an option to turn your present profile page into a fan Page. Just be aware that this is now a public page that anyone can follow. In all my years of social media training, I've always coached people to keep personal and work pages separate. You want everyone to be able to follow your business page but you don't want to let just anyone into your personal life. Facebook has an excellent section in their Help Center on the pros and cons of turning your profile into a business page, and instructions on how to go about it.

I recommend every author have a website, an email list, and a Facebook page. They will help you score the marketing trifecta:

- Discoverability: making it easier for people to find you and your books.
- Engagement: using good content to keep their attention and make them come back for more.
- Connection: building friendships that will encourage loyalty and build word-of-mouth recommendations.

Action Steps

1. Evaluate your website and consider whether you need to update it. Ask a friend to take a look and see what they say.
2. Do you currently have a Facebook Page for your author brand or are you using your personal profile to promote your books? Read the section in the Facebook Help Center on what all is involved in the conversion process: on.fb.me/1GDk91V. Assess the pros and cons of turning your profile into an official Facebook Page. In the first video of the bonus materials, we will explore this issue. Make sure you sign up at the end of the book.
3. Are you currently developing an email list? If not, do some research and planning on how you can use a free program like MailChimp to get started. Schedule time to research the basics of email marketing. Email providers usually have a good library of tutorials to help.

Chapter 14: The Next Three - Pinterest, Author Pages, And Blogs

Some authors enjoy the marketing side of being an author, especially the social media part. If you decide to use social media as part of your marketing strategy, you will need to curb your enthusiasm (or addiction in some cases) for social media as entertainment and approach it more strategically. If you don't, you will be tempted to just use social media willy-nilly without thought to the why of what you are doing. Choose carefully and strategically when tackling a social media platform. An ill-used or neglected social media channel is worse not being there.

Don't get me wrong. If you are already an avid social media user, you have jumped the first hurdle. But falling in love with social media can cloud your judgment about what channels are good for business. Let me give you an example. I don't recommend Twitter as a primary marketing channel for fiction writers even though I love it. I believe it has some drawbacks that I will cover in the next chapter. But if you love Twitter and use it constantly, then by all means stay there and use the channel to build an audience.

1. Pinterest: The Rising Star

Pinterest is an underrated social media tool for authors, especially fiction authors. It is becoming the most powerful image-based marketing tool on the internet for many sectors and I believe book are next. In the last year, Pinterest announced several new features including advertising options and the coming of "Buy Now" buttons for business pages that will enable users to reach followers with direct buy opportunities within the platform. Pinterest is partnering with Apple Pay for this option and I wouldn't be surprised if iBooks partners with Pinterest for direct buy opportunities soon.

Pinterest is already a major commerce channel for big brands such as Nordstrom, Whole Foods, Wayfair, Sephora, and others. Shopify, the popular online store application, has partnered with Pinterest to help personal brands incorporate "buyable pins" into their Pinterest boards. Pinterest is already a viable selling channel with the ability to send followers directly to a book's Amazon page and close a sale. The rich visual catalog format of the channel encourages long visits by users. And it you have good covers, this is an excellent place to show them off.

On Pinterest, users put together groups of images on boards that are similar to photo galleries or albums. Each "pin" on a board is accompanied by a clickable link of the pin's location online. Put your call to action in the comments and you have an easy-to-navigate book catalog. You can upload images from your own computer or pin them from the internet. Many authors are using a combination of boards themed to their books and their personal life. You can invite other people to pin on any board (great for promotions) or leave them closed. Many authors also use Pinterest's secret board function to pin research for their writing.

The beauty of Pinterest is that you don't have to be a photographer to pin images. With Pinterest's "pin-it" button application loaded on your web browser's toolbar, the program recognizes online images on a page and asks you which image you want to pin and which of your boards you want to pin it to. It then gives you an option to edit the information that accompanies the image.

Smart authors will cross-promote Pinterest on other online channels including Facebook, their website, and their email newsletters to build their follower numbers and enhance searchability on Google.

I've seen some very creative author Pinterest sites that include cover reveal boards, bookstores, images of locations from their novels, historic period dress, personal recipes, images from their travels, other authors they recommend, favorite food photos, favorite movies, gardens, images that depict scenes in their books, boards to dedicated to individual books, fan favorites and more. It's a good idea to have a mix of what you like and what your fans will want to see. Confine your book selling to one or two boards.

If your Pinterest page is a personal one, I recommend evolving it into an official business page. Pinterest has a quick system for turning a personal page into a business page that will allow you access to Pinterest's analytics and also enable you to advertise with "promoted pins" and the new Buy Now button when it becomes available. It is possible to start a business page and maintain a separate personal page, but you cannot use the same name for both. You can have secret boards for personal use on your business page and invite the friends you want to share with if you like. More tips on using Pinterest along with some examples of authors using Pinterest can be found in this article: http://bit.ly/1GoJoVC from the Where Writers Win website.

2. Author Pages

Author pages are important enough to be included in The Big Three but they do not require the constant attention of a regular social media platform, email newsletter, or website. In this section I will cover Author Central, Goodreads, and bio pages on other sales platforms. For many fans, this is their first contact with you or your books. Make sure you put your best face forward.

Author Central

If you sell books on Amazon you should be familiar with Author Central. What many authors are not familiar with is the tab called "Author Page". I amazed at the number of authors who are not taking advantage of this great opportunity. The author page is where readers are taken when they click on your name under the title of your book listing on Amazon. Also, if someone searches you by name, your author page should show up near the top of that search.

Amazon lets you populate this page with a wealth of information including a biography, photos, videos, your blog posts, Twitter posts, events, and more. I recommend that authors put links to their website and Facebook page within their biography and mention your newsletter sign up as well. Put each one on a separate line at the end of your biography under a heading such as "Connect With [your name] Here." Make sure you fill out as much as you can and do not forget a profile picture—one where people can see your smiling face. Keep information on this page current.

Author Central also houses your book sales information under the Sales Info tab. Become familiar with how to decipher their data. There is a section on this topic in the help section in Author Central on Amazon.

Goodreads

Goodreads is where readers and authors can talk about what they're reading, join book clubs and interest groups, review books, enter giveaways, advertise, and much more. Technically you can't sell books on Goodreads, but if your book is on Kindle, readers can click on the Preview button on your book's Goodreads page to read a sample. At the bottom of that sample page is a "get full version" button that takes them directly to the book's Kindle page to buy.

As an author you should also be a reader in the Goodreads community. There is a trust factor that develops when people believe you are not just there to sell your books. Readers want to know what you're reading. Michelle Campbell-Scott has written a comprehensive and easy-to-use guide called *Goodreads For*

Authors, which I recommend. It starts out with the basics and moves to more advanced techniques, so it is easy to implement as you go.

A word of caution: There has been some discussion about whether authors should reach out to reviewers through Goodreads messaging. Since Amazon has been cracking down on "friends that review" books, it might be a good idea to develop your advance reader team by regular email channels or your Facebook group rather than by Goodreads messaging. There is no evidence that Amazon's bots are monitoring Goodreads, but they do own the platform. I recommend reaching out to reviewers who have positively reviewed your books on Goodreads and asking them if they are interested in reviewing other books. However, give them an email address and ask them to contact you there.

Other Book Sales Platforms

Wherever you sell your books online, make sure you fill out an author profile that includes the URL of your website, an invitation to join your newsletter (especially if you offer a free book as an incentive), and the URL of your Facebook page. The heading may say biography, but don't forget to take advantage of that important real estate for telling people how they can connect with you.

3. To Blog or Not to Blog

I struggled with whether I should include blogging in this section over Twitter, but blogs have so many advantages over Twitter for discoverability and content longevity that blogging won out. It is a better platform than Twitter for by far for fiction writers. If you are a nonfiction author, Twitter is probably a must as well as blogging.

You would think that writers would love to blog, but many do not. I have seen too many blogs started and then abandoned. It's better to not start until you can make a solid commitment to the time it takes to produce enough good content to be viable. If you want to have an ==effective blog, you need to post at least once a week.== This sounds daunting, but I follow authors who blog three or four times a week.

The ideal blog post length is negotiable depending on the content. You don't need 1200 words to feature an image quote. It can be a blog piece by itself, especially around book launch time. I believe short is better for fiction writers. The exception would be if you are publishing a short story or publishing a short excerpt from your book. Nonfiction writers may need longer pieces of 1200 to 1800 words if their content is designed to establish expertise.

Blog posts have a strong discoverability advantage in search engines if your blog has a dedicated domain (e.g. www.yourname.com). You can implement a blog plugin like Yoast which helps you optimize your blog entries for search without having to be an expert in search engine optimization (SEO). Blog content also has longevity—it is housed at one location indefinitely to be searched and shared by new readers that find your blog. If you like blogging, there are likely many opportunities to guest blog for other authors. This exposes your brand to a new audience. Most blogging platforms support email subscriptions as well which deliver every new post directly to a follower's inbox.

Even though social media experts like Buffer say the ideal blog length is 1600 words, short-form content can also be effective. Jay Baer calls this "snackable content." Fiction bloggers can keep it shorter because followers are seeking "entertaining content" rather than "instructive content". Think images, infographics, 15-second videos, image quotes, illustrated travelogue diary entries, guest posts by fan reviewers, news stories of fun events, bios of your characters, or short book reviews of other authors' works. You can also cross-promote your blog content easily on all your social media channels including your website.

I recommend auto feeding your blog entries to Facebook via your blog's dashboard or connect your blog to Networked Blogs (https://www.facebook.com/networkedblogs) which will publish it automatically if you wish. I also recommend uploading your blog posts to a Pinterest board dedicated to that purpose. See my example here: http://bit.ly/1MnHF9C. Include at least one image with every blog post to make sure it can be pinned. You can also create content by inviting guest bloggers, but make sure you count the time cost to invite, edit, and schedule. If you are a nonfiction writer you should also be posting your blog writing on LinkedIn publishing platform..

The biggest downside of a blog is the time it takes to find and produce content. You are doing the bare minimum if you produce just once per week. There are many creative ways to promote your writing while entertaining readers, but the sheer time commitment scares many people. It's also tough to build a robust following on a blog without cross-promotion on social media. Using a blogging platform such as Medium or Tumblr offers very little discovery benefits unless you write books specifically to their target demographics: young adults and new adults. As I mentioned in the previous chapter, I believe WordPress is the best platform for developing a multi-functional website and blog. You can host a blog at WordPress.com for free and have a pretty professional-looking blog. Just a note that a free WordPress site sets a limit on how much media (pictures, video) you can save on their servers. Also, most of the high-functioning plugins do not work on free sites.

If you want more bells and whistles, use a lot of images and video, or want to include a store option, I would recommend a WordPress.org website for your blog where you have to subscribe to hosting with a company like Bluehost. The capacity for options is much larger when you are on the paid platform.

Action Steps

1. Do you have an updated profile on Goodreads and Author Central that includes a profile picture (smiling face shot)? If not, make a plan to do that this week. Of all the platforms in this chapter, these two take the least amount of time for the value they return. Take some time to explore both platforms and see what options are available. Make a plan to check in on both regularly, especially Goodreads. Don't forget to reference all your social media outposts and email sign-up in your bio section, especially if you use perma-free books to entice email sign-ups.

2. If you don't have a blog, find some authors in your genre who do maintain blogs and follow a couple. See how much work goes into maintaining a blog and count the cost before you set one up. You should figure on publishing a minimum of once per week.

Chapter 15: The Playground - How Much Social Media Is Enough?

When I was in elementary school, I loved the playground. After I ate lunch, I couldn't wait to get out there for the 30-minute break. Our playground had kickball diamonds, foursquare courts, dodge ball courts, a huge grassy field in addition to a mind-blowing selection of swings, teeter-totters, monkey bars, merry-go-rounds, areas for hopscotch and jump roping, tether ball, and much more. The options were overwhelming but delightful.

This section of the toolbox is like a playground: lots to choose from, but you want to choose the tools that are a good fit for your strategy. Here we will look at blogging, Twitter, podcasts, live video, Instagram, Snapchat, and mobile apps.

These are the tools that you have to love to use because the return in discoverability or sales may be lower than the amount of work you have to put in. Having said that, these are also the channels where some authors have invested followings. Another title for this chapter might be *Take It Or Leave It*. Each of these sections is divided into three parts based on the platform's ability to aid discoverability, build a target audience, and sell more books:
- Strengths
- Weaknesses
- Who might want to use it.

There are some differences in my recommendations in this chapter based on whether you write fiction or nonfiction.

Twitter

Twitter is included in this chapter based solely on its usefulness to fiction writers. I know this is controversial but I have my reasons why I think Twitter is not a go-to platform for fiction sales. If you are a nonfiction or a hybrid writer, Twitter should be a Big Three priority for you, even over Facebook. Especially if you blog. I have include information for nonfiction writers in the *Who Might Use It* section, so hang in there with me.

Strengths: Twitter is a real-time news channel. It is all about what is happening now. Twitter users check their feeds more frequently than their Facebook pages. Twitter is a news conduit. It is also an excellent place to curate and search content on a topic. Hashtags (#) become gathering points for people following topics and trends. Twitter also makes a good back channel for conversation during a live event such as a TV show or a professional conference. If you use Twitter as a business brand, there are several types of Twitter cards you can use to highlight different types of content and grab more attention (https://dev.twitter.com/cards/overview).

Weaknesses: The fact that tweets are fighting for eyeballs on a crowded highway in real-time means that to use it for discoverability, you need to tweet probably 4-6 times a day at minimum. The content lifespan on Twitter is not very long without retweets. Research shows that the majority of retweets happen in the first hour, so your content fades quickly. If you don't use lists to aggregate people in topic feeds, you can spend 15 minutes trying to get through 60 seconds of the latest tweets. The noise level on Twitter is deafening.

Even though Twitter does allow photos, they are often awkwardly cropped. If you want to share a lot of photos, make sure you know the size of the preview hole so your news feed images are not causing people to move on. Make sure the most eye-catching piece of the image shows in the preview. Last but not least, Twitter only commands 23 percent of the online adults in the United States according to Pew Internet. And 37 percent of those users are under 29 years old. You might argue that Pinterest has similar numbers. The culture on Pinterest is different—it is a browsing channel set up to lend itself to commerce. Its content has more longevity than Twitter. That culture is a huge difference maker.

Who might want to use Twitter: If you are already very active on Twitter, use it. Don't be afraid to sell, but keep in mind that Twitter's strength is providing information in the middle of the sales funnel, not closing the sale (see Chapter 18). If you become too salesy on Twitter, you will turn into background noise. If your writing hits Twitter's age demographic, such as young adult or new adult fiction, you have more prospective followers there. I recommend following the content of influencers in that age group first so you get the hang of how to effectively speak their language. If you are doing research for a book, Twitter has a strong search function. Learn how to use it well (https://support.twitter.com/articles/132700), and also set up lists around content areas for easier reference: (https://support.twitter.com/articles/76460). Lists make referencing people and topics much less time consuming.

Nonfiction writers should consider Twitter. Count on more maintenance than Facebook or Pinterest. Connecting on Twitter effectively means being present four or more times a day to tweet, check notifications, and peruse your lists. You can use Twitter to help establish your expertise by gathering links to helpful information you find online and tweeting them to followers. Also, cross-promote your blog articles and website there. Follow prospects as well as other experts in your field. Be generous with favorites—use them as thank-you nods—and honor the reciprocal culture by retweeting others, even your competition. To succeed on Twitter, you can't have a scarcity mentality. Just from personal experience, I know more nonfiction writers that have success selling on Twitter than fiction writers. But my experience isn't research, so if your experience is different, keep calm and carry on.

Instagram

Strengths: Instagram is soaring in popularity with younger demographics. The platform has made it clear that it is pursuing e-commerce and advertising possibilities. Because Instagram is owned by Facebook, I expect to see more changes in these areas sooner than later. You can now schedule ads on Instagram through Facebook's Ads Manager dashboard. Images and video are Instagram's strong point. Instagram recently added more options in their screen size dimensions to favor the size of most video and camera screens. Good images can make an emotional connection with followers. Emphasis on good.

Weaknesses: I am not convinced that Instagram is a good marketing channel for authors… yet. Its ad platform is in development. At present, in order to embed links with images you need to purchase a third-party service that is pretty pricey. So, your only chance to embed a promotional link is in your profile or as a dead link in the comments section of the photo. Only hashtags are live links in Instagram comments.

Search is another conundrum on Instagram. Profiles can be searched on Google, but searching for someone using Instagram's search can be difficult if you don't know the name on their profile. People tend to use cryptic names or their Twitter usernames on Instagram as the platform does not require real names as Facebook does (supposedly).

Who Might Use Instagram: If you write for teens or publish books that have visual context such as cookbooks, you may want to consider Instagram. Be careful of using Instagram for personal and business on the same account. Teens who follow you as an author will probably not engage with pictures of your grandchildren or vacations. If you are a nonfiction writer and publish cookbooks or other visual genres, Instagram would be a good bet. Study other authors in your genre on Instagram to see what kind of content gets a lot of likes and comments.

Snapchat

I personally like Snapchat. I was working in higher education marketing when Snapchat first came out, and I had some clients who had success engaging student audiences. I use it personally but don't recommend it for book marketing.

Strengths: Its popularity is its biggest strength. It has a firm grip in the teen sector. If you are a creative and love doodling, you might have some fun with Snapchat. And fun is really where it's at with Snapchat.

Weaknesses: Because many people don't understand the unique strengths and weaknesses of Snapchat, there is a wealth of ho-hum content there. Instead of being innovative, the bulk of people there are just imitating the poor content of others. It is definitely a storytelling platform. Its vertical-only orientation can be a drag. Prepare to be producing content on a regular basis to gain followers. Snapchat stories completely disappear in 24 hours and there is no archive for viewers to search. I think Snapchat content is highly forgettable. It's a tricky channel to use for marketing.

Who Might Use Snapchat: If you write for teens and want to consider Snapchat I recommend following brands there first. Set up a Snapchat profile and search for some well-known brands that do a good job. Start by following these usernames: dabttll, disneyland, fallontonight, fathermarquette, hailstatesnap, mashable, mcdonalds, mls, mplatco, shonduras, tacobell, and teamsnapchat.

Video and Live Streaming

Video rocks social media if done well. The trouble is, it takes some learning. Live streaming is very popular at this writing as Meerkat, Periscope, and Blab are just starting to take off. But good live video requires some equipment, some learning, and time to plan and produce.

Strengths: If done well, live video can facilitate the closest thing we have to a face-to-face connection in social media. Periscope has a bit of a promotion advantage in that you can automatically follow people on Periscope that you follow on Twitter. Also, Periscope recently added the ability to shoot horizontally giving users a wider screen. Periscope also has archive ability. Applications such as Katch will capture your broadcasts and you can upload them to a YouTube or Vimeo channel.

Weaknesses: People are still struggling with live video. Honestly, some people do not belong on camera. Video is the most unforgiving channel—every physical flaw, bad facial expression, monotone voice, or fumbling for words is a turnoff. Bad lighting and poor audio will kill video. Once upon a time people were fascinated with video of any quality. Now they have a low tolerance for crap. Make sure to educate yourself on the best practices of online video before you venture in.

Who Might Use Video: If you already have the equipment or can piece it together with a small budget, you might want to consider video. The biggest hurdle is the time and expertise it takes to actually produce good video. Follow people who are doing live video well by searching Google for "best people on Periscope." I recommend doing some online research to see if you have the time, resources, and skill to dive in. Just make sure it fits one of your marketing goals.

Podcasts

Do you like to talk? How pleasant is your voice? I learned years ago while working in radio that being engaging with audio alone is harder than it looks. Listen to some popular author podcasts if you are considering a podcast. There is a short list of recommendations in Chapter 20.

Weaknesses: There are several challenges with podcasting. First, there will be an equipment cost depending on how fancy you want to get with microphones and production software. Podcast audiences seem to have the least tolerance for irregularity. You need to produce a regular show. Podcasts also require good cohesive content. Building a subscriber base is difficult but not impossible.

Publishing, hosting, and uploading your podcasts to subscription services like iTunes, Podcast Addict, Stitcher, and others take some learning. I recommend downloading a free ebook from HubSpot on how to start a podcast here: http://blog.hubspot.com/marketing/how-to-start-podcast.

Strengths: Nonfiction and hybrid writers (fiction and nonfiction) will have a much easier task building a podcast audience. Again, attention spans are shorter for entertainment content than instructive content. Your podcast can be as short as five minutes but probably not longer than 60. I recommend putting together a template for your shows so listeners can expect the same type of content every week. If you have a large network of fellow authors, you might consider a podcast based on guest interviews.

Podcasts are portable. People can listen to podcasts on multiple devices including their laptops, phones, tablets, and even on their car radios. My car has a Stitcher app loaded in its radio which has extended my podcast listening quite a bit. People can listen while exercising at the gym, walking, doing housework, answering email, or driving a car.

Who Might Want to Podcast: Nonfiction and hybrid writers might want to consider a podcast. The biggest key with podcasts is regularity. Can you produce a show on a schedule? Finding a content niche is going to be another need with a podcast. Generic "how to write better" podcasts have little value. If you have a special talent or Jedi trick nobody else has you may be able to parlay that into a podcast. Do your research and find out what is out there. Can you fill a gap?

If you are the kind of person who likes the playground, do your research before you jump in. Run your ideas through the SMART filter: make sure it is sustainable, manageable, audience-specific, relevant, and strategic, not just tactical.

How much social is too much social? That depends on who you are and how natural the marketing process is for you. For some, just getting the Big Three in line is going to be an arduous task. For others, the more the better. The only reminder I have is this: social media can be a lot of fun, but not all social media will help you sell books and build a loyal audience. If you have time to play, then go for it. Maybe it energizes you. Just be careful that your play doesn't hamper your work. Always consider the why first.

Action Steps

1. Pick out one channel in this chapter that interests you. Now, using the strengths and weaknesses, make a list of how each one applies to you. Do you fit in the "who might want to use this channel" category? Brainstorm with your schedule. Do you have the time for a learning curve or would it be better to skip it for now?

Part IV - The SMART Campaign — It's All About Momentum

As I write this, the presidential election in the U.S. is over a year away. But presidential hopefuls are already vying for social media influence with ads, promoted posts, and campaigns to build their follower numbers. Their savvy marketing people know that momentum is the key to winning the social media election. The more buzz you build, the more successful your campaign will be.

Chapter 16: What Is A Campaign?

A marketing campaign is a series of strategies designed to reach a goal in a defined period of time. Your marketing goals are part of your long-term strategy: building a mailing list or promoting a backlist of books already published. Short-term campaigns are standalone projects like book launches. A short-term campaign has four definite phases: planning, pre-launch, launch, and follow-through.

Campaign marketing is often misunderstood. Sometimes people believe a short-term campaign will command an automatic audience because it is a special event. The truth is, if you build awareness going into a campaign, the momentum can boost your results. So before we dive any deeper into this section we need to take a look at the success formula: campaign success is proportional to the reach (numbers) and advocacy level of your current fan base multiplied by your momentum. Without that momentum, your campaigns may be seen as a rude interruption.

Campaigns Have Unique Characteristics:

1. You can break posting frequency rules during a campaign. If your fans see you as a friend, they will cut you some slack during short-term campaigns. If you have a one-day event and let your fans know, you can post more often on your social media outlets promoting the event without danger of losing your loyal fans. People know you are going to sell at some point, and they don't mind you doing so provided you are giving them enough valuable content to balance out the selling. They may not all be ready to buy, but they won't unsubscribe in droves when you post more than usual during a campaign. They know what they signed up for.

2. Campaigns can reap benefits besides sales. If your campaigns have contests or giveaways, you can tie participation to an action such as commenting, using a hashtag, or asking people to like a post that promotes your email sign-up. Contests can create a hype that brings new fans to your page or increases email sign-ups for free books. Just make sure to use wisdom and follow the contest rules on every channel. Book launches also give you opportunities to promote other books, especially if they are part of a series. Think creatively about how you can use a campaign to help reach other long-term goals.

3. Campaigns need value propositions for maximum impact. A value proposition is a fancy phrase that asks what value your campaign offers to fans. The answer to the question "what's in it for me" should be evident to your fans. I have one client who runs two thank-you campaigns every year with a goal of increasing her social media numbers—one around the December holiday season for her Facebook group and another in July for fans of her Facebook page. The two events have multiple prize packages given away around a theme where participants have to take a social action (comment, like a post, add to a Pinterest board, sign up for a newsletter, or retweet) to enter the daily giveaways. It's the highest time of engagement on both of her pages.

4. Campaigns that have a successful pre-launch have a better chance of success. Campaign success is accelerated if you step on the gas pedal leading up to the launch. It's all about momentum. Build anticipation before an event and people will be primed to take an action. The pre-launch phase needs to be short—a month, tops. I've done successful pre-launches that were only ten days out. The key to success is planning.

Action Steps

1. Do you set up planned campaigns to launch your books? If not, how do you think your sales could benefit from a planned campaign?

Chapter 17: The Four Phases Of Short-Term Campaigns
The Planning Phase

Short-term campaigns have four necessary stages for success: ==planning, pre-launch, launch, and follow-through.== When planning a short-term campaign, start with a calendar. I suggest you plan all your launches and short-term campaigns on an annual cycle, if possible. Whether you have a planning calendar application or just use a spreadsheet, an annual plan makes sure your campaigns will not overlap and burn out your fans. They need a break from selling messages. However, that doesn't mean you never sell anything outside a campaign. Since campaigns elevate the noise level on your social media channels, you need to give people spans of time to feel normal as well..

Campaign dates need to be chosen with wisdom. Is there a major holiday time or event you want to piggyback or stay away from? When are your highest book sales? After you have chosen your campaign dates for the year, you need to use that same calendar or spreadsheet to schedule your planning times. After you set a launch date for a campaign, you work backwards on the calendar to know when planning and pre-launch phases should begin. This might sound daunting at first, but using this system will reap rewards once you get started. Using a calendar to book your campaigns will help ensure that your marketing is manageable.

Your planning phase is the most important of all phases. This is where you put together a GOST campaign plan from Chapter 7. Keep in mind other time commitments so you don't overwhelm your schedule. If I am doing a book launch, I start working on the planning phase three months or more ahead of time. Even though I usually don't start a pre-launch until a month before the launch, I design, write, and put together everything I will need during the planning phase. I will spend chunks of time here and there to get the work done so I can keep writing, blogging, and doing life. Once I have a template for a campaign, it is easy to judge how long tasks will take the next time. The first time is always the hardest.

How much time you spend on planning is dictated by the size of your campaign. If you're just starting out, I recommend keeping it simple. In the bonus materials that come with the book, I'll show you how to plan a simple, beginner level book launch campaign that allows time for you to still write and have a regular life.

Planning for a Multi-Audience Campaign

You will want to prepare content aimed at three groups of readers during your short-term campaign:

Audience #1: People on your email list: They are your most invested group. They have already given you permission to send them promotional emails. Most of them probably follow you somewhere on social media as well. I usually prepare three emails for this group during the month before the launch. The first goes out a month ahead and is a save-the-date sort of message that lets them know I will be sending them exclusive information about the new book (or event) in the coming weeks. The other two go out at five days, and launch day. The five day email usually has a special feature that gives a sneak peek at the content or an image quote. I've seen a number of these types of email schedules for product launches and you just have to find the schedule that works best for your followers.

Your pre-launch schedule for this group is influenced by how often you publish. If you write four or more books a year you will want to shorten that to two emails: save the date and launch day. If you are running any giveaways during your launch, make sure your newsletter people know where to go to participate. The rest of your year should be business as usual with your email list: send them regular helpful newsletters or offers.

Audience #2: Your social media followers: They have opted to get your content in their news feeds by following you. To heighten their anticipation of an event, I recommend a giveaway promotion leading up to the launch on Facebook that is cross-promoted on your other channels including your blog and website. Contests make your followers pay closer attention. Include some calls-to-action in these posts and possible boost an important post to get more reach. In the planning phase, I put together the giveaway cycle and get messages and images ready in addition to putting a few prize packages together. Facebook has some apps designed for running contests and giveaways that you can access in the menu on the left column of your Home page under the Apps heading. Also, check out Facebook's rules for promotions by searching "promotion guidelines" in Facebook's Help Center.

Audience #3: Readers who don't follow you yet: You also want content that reaches new readers during the campaign. This is where you may want to run Facebook ads, buy a cover ad on a review site, or put together a social media ambassador campaign for your followers. Social media ambassadors, also called a street team, can be a valuable resource in recruiting new fans.

You'll want to give your social media ambassadors some pre-made digital content they can share on all their social media channels. You can house all the content you will ask people to share on a website page, including images, sample tweets, Facebook posts and images for Pinterest, on a book page you put together on your website. That way you can direct ambassadors to a place where they can grab something pre-made to share on their social media.

The Pre-Launch Phase

A pre-launch starts anywhere from ten days to two months or more before a book launch. During your planning phase you will have put together all your graphics, drafted all your email blasts, put together a book page on your website, sent inquiries out to potential reviewers, secured endorsements, enlisted a launch team, and have all your tactics scheduled on the calendar for pre-launch, launch, and follow-through. It all depends on the elements in your launch plan. Just remember that the calendar is a work in progress. I don't think I've ever done a book launch, or any campaign for that matter, where the dates I put down in the planning phase all worked like clockwork. Stuff happens.

Keep in mind whatever you do in this phase is about building momentum. There are a number of proven strategies authors have used during pre-launch including giveaways and contests on their social media channels, excerpt releases on blogs, guest appearances on other author blogs, appearances on podcasts, Facebook ads, book cover ads on respected review sites, email blasts, and many more.

Make sure the lifespan of your content is a match for your goals. For instance, Facebook ads can span any amount of time you stipulate, but I recommend designing ads specifically for pre-launch, launch, and follow-through if you have a budget for advertising. Month-long book cover ads on review sites and guest blogs have discoverability beyond their initial appearance, but Facebook parties and email blasts have short-term impact and should be saved for closer to the actual launch. If you want to see how elaborate a nonfiction pre-launch can be, read this piece on how Jay Baer set aside a year to launch his bestseller, *Youtility*:http://bit.ly/1QPE5nB.

The Launch Phase

If you've prepared well, the rocket should take off smoothly. Once you push the launch button, the phase becomes more about monitoring and gauging feedback to see if adjustments need to be made. I'll give you an example. Let's say I have two Facebook ads scheduled, which I always do. I like to do what marketers call A/B testing—running two similar ads at the same time with subtle differences—to see which one gets better traction. Maybe they have different audiences or different images. I will monitor those ads and if one takes off, I will pull the other and put more money into the successful ad. I also want to monitor my social media posts. I have clients who do reviewer excerpts on Facebook during the launch period. Often, one of them will take off and it is a perfect candidate for a Promoted Post (more on that later). But for the most part, right now is about executing the plan.

Here are some examples of launch phase activities:

1. Fulfill your guest blog and podcast responsibilities on the launch calendar. Promote your appearances and publicly thank your hosts afterwards.
2. Mail out prizes awarded during pre-launch.
3. Monitor ads and promotions to track upticks in sales making allowances for a promotion's life. For instance, tweets have almost no extended life and they are not searchable on Google. Even when they are shared, their life expectancy is still low. Repetition and well-written posts are the keys to more life. Podcasts, guest blogs, and interviews have more life because they are not necessarily accessed in real time. A cover ad on a review site is usually up for a month.
4. Check to make sure review team members have posted their reviews and send personal thank-yous to those that have.
5. Adjust the frequency of planned social media posts if necessary.
6. Add to the shared assets page as needed.
7. Be present regularly on your social media channels to ask questions and thank fans for their support.
8. Keep writing and doing life.

The launch phase of a book usually lasts about two to three weeks. Your promotions should include a reduction in social media traffic after the first and second weeks and eventually returning to a normal rate before the follow-up phase. If you publish a book every three or four months, I recommend a two-week launch period. If you don't publish as frequently, you may want to schedule launch activities for a month or longer.

The Follow-Up Phase

The most important thing to remember about the follow-through: be mindful of all the new followers, subscribers, and loyal fans you have gained. If your launch went as planned you should have heightened engagement and increased numbers on your social channels right now. By the time your follow-up starts, your social media posting frequencies should have returned to normal, but now you need to add another piece to your marketing mix: introducing your new followers to your brand.

Remember that new followers need nurturing to stay invested, so save some of your "best stuff" for the follow-up period. This is also a key time to show value to your loyal fans so new followers can see much you appreciate your supporters. If you have done giveaways during the launch, I recommend sending a written thank-you note with each gift you mail out asking winners to post a picture on your Facebook page or group when they receive their goodies in the mail. I also recommend using a mix of fan-oriented content during this time that may include the following tactics:

1. Produce short video thank-yous to dedicated fans who helped you launch your book. You can use your phone to produce these. You can post these short videos on your Facebook page and also on Twitter. Make sure you tag the person in the video—yes, I learned this by experience.

2. Don't forget to thank those people who hosted guest posts and podcasts with a public shout-out on social media and a link recommending their blog.

3. Schedule a follow-up email to everyone who signed up for your newsletter during your launch campaign. If you use an email provider like AWeber, schedule this before your pre-launch so everyone gets it right after they sign-up. Maybe you have a perma-free book you can give them as a bonus. Also include links to all your social media channels and invite new people to connect with you there.

4. Review excerpts from fans are good post-launch social media. You can drop these into Canva templates and make them into an image.

5. Remember your marketing mix from Chapter 10. Get back to adding value.

6. Give shout-outs on your social media channels to new followers.

7. If you made social media cover photos promoting your book launch, change the cover to reflect the book is now "the latest release".

8. Keep asking for reviews in your newsletter and on your social media channels.

9. Cross-promote links to all your social media channels for a couple weeks so new followers know where else they can connect with you.

10. Stay vigilant when replying to messages on all your social media platforms and author pages. Return phone calls promptly and answer your emails. There is no rest, just a change of routine.

I recommend that a follow-up phase last two weeks. At some point during the follow-up, business will return to "normal" and you'll probably be well into writing your next book. Just remember your work is not done. In his book *20,000 Days And Counting*, author Robert Smith says, "You never really cross the finish line. Accomplishing a big goal [like writing a book] isn't the finish line, it's the new starting line."

Action Steps

1. How many books do you publish a year? If it is more than three, how would adjust your pre-launch and post-launch phases so you don't over saturate your fan base with content?

2. Brainstorm what types of events besides book launches would qualify as short-term marketing campaigns in your marketing mix.

Chapter 18: The SMART Way To Use Paid Online Ads To Boost Sales

One thing I love about living in rural America is the food. Don't get me wrong, I love urban dining. But nothing beats a hearty meal prepared in a traditional farm kitchen. That's where comfort food got its name. In her glory days, my mother-in-law was the model of farm cookery and her specialty was the hot dish. My mom used to call them casseroles. These are not the Hamburger Helper variety, they are homemade goodness in a casserole dish. A good hot dish is a marvelous concoction of tastes and textures.

One of my favorite hot dish recipes is called the Cowboy Dinner. It's a recipe so easy, even a cowboy could make it. It has layers of cooked hamburger, frozen peas, canned tomato soup, sliced potatoes, canned cream of mushroom soup, chopped onions and celery, shredded cheese, and whatever else you wanted to throw in. If I went through the dozen or so local cookbooks on my shelf, I know I could find at least ten variations of a Cowboy Dinner. They all taste good, I'm sure, but the recipes are all different. When I think of social media advertising, it reminds me a lot of that hot dish: one name, many different ingredients.

The Elephant in the Room: Measurable Results

There are very few things in book marketing more frustrating than trying to prove that social media advertising sells books. Sometimes it does, sometimes it doesn't. It's the "doesn't" part that frustrates authors. But, if we knew which types of ads are designed to sell what when, and which are not, it would help. If we knew which social media channels lend themselves to selling and which do not, that would help even more. But one word of warning: if you try to use sales as the only measurement for social media ads, you are missing other important benefits. The key is learning how to take a goal or objective and design an ad campaign that can accomplish that goal. If your only goal is sales, social media won't be a big help. You can sell books on social media if you know what you're doing—lots of books. But keep in mind that social media is not a bookstore. It's not Amazon, or Kobo, or iTunes.

First, paid advertising online requires some knowledge about advertising in general. Let's take a quick tour.

The Man in the Middle Is Social Media

Marketers talk a lot about the sales funnel. Some believe the sales funnel has changed significantly since social media became mainstream, but traditional practices of qualifying buyers with content and stages of buying still apply no matter what the funnel looks like. The sales funnel is designed to move people from the top to the bottom—sometimes quickly, and sometimes it takes a while. Here's the traditional sales funnel:

The sales funnel describes the traditional buying cycle. What has changed the most is that the middle three stages of the funnel, *opinion*, *consideration*, and *preference*, take place almost completely online today. Before the internet, people had to rely on salespeople, companies, and ads to give them that information. Now, people are gathering their own information from review websites, social media recommendations, and other resources that are out of the hands of the sellers. The cycle can be accelerated or disrupted depending on the product information people gather and their motivation to buy.

The conundrum with social media ads came to light in a recent AOL Platforms study that showed social media has very little impact on the first and last phase of the sales funnel. According to the study, YouTube had the most impact in the first two phases (32%) and last phase (14%). In general, all social media platforms had less than a 15% impact on the final buy phase of a sale. Facebook was second to YouTube when it came to impacting a buy at 10%, Pinterest at 8%, and Twitter at 4%. You can see that none of these figures are stellar. Social media is strongest in the middle—the delivering of information after awareness and before the sale. No wonder social media ads can be a bust if you are expecting it to sell a boatload of books.

So Why Bother?

Every day I come across authors who use social media to sell books. They brag about it, write case studies about it, give you their numbers, and tell you to spend your money on social media ads. I am not going to do that. Social media ads can sell a consistent number of books if you are publishing the right content, and more if your books are already popular, but it is not a main sales channel *at this time*. If someone tells you they are selling hundreds of books with Facebook ads, they are probably selling thousands elsewhere. But selling books is only one of the benefits of using Facebook ads. They are excellent vehicles for building an email list if done correctly. It's the "correctly" part that trips people up.

Social media is meant to foster connection and build community which will give you a broader sales platform over time. It's an organic medium. That means it's tough to game the system with thousands of tweets in a week.

But let me just say this: people can have *outlier success* where they had just the right combination of being in the right place at the right time with the right message, but had no strategy or goals. Their success is an anomaly and should be treated that way, not copied. A word of caution: use wisdom when you duplicate case studies you find on successful Facebook or Twitter advertising campaigns. Unless you have a very similar set of parameters including budget, you will need to scale your goals and expectations.

For instance, author Mark Dawson teaches a successful class on how to build an email using Facebook ads from his business, Self Publishing Formula. Mark has quite a robust budget—one many indies will not be able to duplicate. But you can scale his ideas using realistic goals and an affordable budget and you can have success, but on a different scale.

So why bother? Because you *can* learn how to use paid advertising successfully to sell more books, build and email list, and promote an event. But there will be a learning curve and some trial and error. The biggest question marks in online advertising are audience targeting and budget. If you can find the sweet spot, you will succeed.

Most people fail because their expectations are not based on reality. Your return will suffer if you try and force a Facebook ad to do something it cannot accomplish. For instance, I had a client that once tried to give her email list a boost by running a giveaway that coincided with a popular holiday. She wanted to give away one of her popular books by asking people to join her email list to get the book. Her ad ran for 24 hours and our acquisition cost was a whopping $4.50 per subscriber gained. That is not good. After evaluating the campaign and acquisition cost we decided:

- A 24-hour ad was not built for the result we were expecting. Building an email list with Facebook ads is a long-term project that requires a decent budget. The key is not about how much money you have to spend, it is in acquisition costs.
- Our ad was not as visually appealing as it should be. We tried to use the book cover in the ad and with the landscape orientation of Facebook ads, it wasn't as exciting as it should have been.

Lastly, I have personally found that successful Facebook campaigns can boost an email list much quicker than a sign-up promotion in the front and back matter of your books or a widget on your website. But ideally you need all your email sign-up forms in as many highly visible locations as possible if you are serious about building your email list.

What Are You Aiming For?

If you have a long-term plan to use social media for marketing, be aware that you need to understand how to measure if your content is hitting your goals. Jay Baer, one of my favorite social media experts, penned a guide on how to measure content success in 2012 that is still a standard of measurement today. In the piece, Baer pinpointed "four types of metrics that matter" and explained why we need to be pursuing and measuring all four:

1. **Consumption metrics:** These are the easiest metrics to set up, measure, and explain. They answer the question of how many people viewed, downloaded or listened to this piece of content. Almost every platform will give you this data, from email to YouTube to Facebook to Google and so on. Unfortunately, this is the level where a lot of marketers quit. These metrics also have the least value in predicting a sale but do help us get a handle on awareness. A basic consumption metric would be a like, favorite, or heart.
2. **Sharing metrics:** How often is this content shared with others? Measuring shares helps determine engagement and awareness. It can also help you identify potential ambassadors. These include shares, retweets, repins, forwards, and sharing links.
3. **Lead generation metrics:** Most often used in the business world, these metrics show that people are ready to hear from you—they identify readers at the next stage of the buying cycle. They have taken a step and filled out a form, signed up for a subscription, or left a comment on a blog. These people are now in need of nurturing—they have given you permission to market to them. They are willing, for the most part, to be sold something. They may not buy, but they are ready to hear directly from you.
4. **Sales metrics:** These are sales made directly through social media. If you don't have an e-commerce store directly hooked to a trackable buy button, you can measure these with the help of Google Analytics, a measurement pixel embedded on a page with a dedicated URL. At the present, only Facebook is offering sales directly from a social media store on their platform, but that option is not yet available to everyone. Selling directly via social media is in its infancy stages, but referral sales are vibrant. Referral sales are

links that are one click away from a direct sale such as an Amazon buy link in a Facebook ad, Twitter card, tweet, or Pinterest pin. Direct sales from social media sales are the most difficult sales to track.

Depending on your goal, you can measure your success with metrics from one of those categories. If you want to build an email list with Facebook ads, the number of new subscribers generated by that ad campaign would be a lead generation metric. If you want to build awareness for your brand or your books, new likes and followers over a specific time period would be a consumption metric. If you want to sell an online class that is an offshoot of your nonfiction book, enrollments from a landing page or a form on social media would be a sales metric.

The Value of Using Social Media to Sell

At this time, selling is not social media's strong suit. It can do some pretty amazing things, but you will never sell as many books via social media as you will through Amazon, Kobo, iTunes or Barnes and Noble. As I said earlier, social media is not a store... yet. When platforms do get their e-commerce ducks in a row, social selling will be a lot more lucrative. But unless Amazon cooperates, and we all know what the answer to that is, it will always be a secondary channel. But honestly, who doesn't want additional sales outlets? No sale is an island. People came to the bookstore from somewhere, and it all adds up. Part of the problem I see now happens when people expect more than social media can actually deliver.

The biggest benefit of social media is that it builds loyalty, word-of-mouth promotion, and awareness like nothing else out there. I know there are a lot of platform-building naysayers, but social media's biggest value is building an audience that wants your product. They are only a click away. Launch teams can be built and nurtured on social media, and so can advance reader teams and reviews. Email lists that directly reach your fans can be created on social media channels. These are all benefits that equate to sales.

One of the objections authors have about social media selling is based on the idea that if it isn't connected to Amazon, it is worthless. Indie authors live in constant fear of what Amazon will do next. Building a community through online media that includes a website, an email list, and a Facebook page may be the only thing you have a couple years from now. What if Amazon yanks your ability to sell or chokes your royalties down so tight your income is negligible? Yeah, I'd get busy building a platform now.

So What Works?

I don't know if I can answer that question to everyone's satisfaction, but I can tell you how social media can help you sell more books. In this section, I'll run through some options that I have used to help clients sell more books—not boatloads—but enough to make it a good channel for selling. I'll share what has worked and what has failed. This is stuff you can test, but again, you need to do it strategically.

Facebook Ads

I have used Facebook ads to sell books during launch week, to build email lists, to increase follower numbers on Facebook and other platforms, and also to occasionally promote backlist books. To succeed with Facebook ads, you need to find the right target audience. It can't just be anybody between the ages of 18 and 70. Learning how to target audiences in Facebook ads is a skill, but it is a learned skill. You are going to need to educate yourself on the following:

- The rules and guidelines for selling on Facebook change regularly. If you are interested in keeping up, you should read the current Facebook advertising guide from Facebook: http://on.fb.me/1MGOu77. And "read" means treat as a textbook. You want to be able to understand the advantages and disadvantages of each type of ad and where they are best suited. Currently, besides Promoted Posts, you have ten different types to choose from. Learn everything you can. Take Mark Dawson's free course on how Facebook ads can build your email list—search for the current link to his course on selfpublishingformula.com. The course is especially valuable for understanding the basics of the Power Editor interface. To keep up on changes and get expert tips, follow Jon Loomer's blog at jonloomer.com. His material skews towards people who already know the basics of Facebook advertising but it will accelerate your learning curve.
- You may have to spend some money experimenting on Facebook ads until you get the hang of it. Don't be discouraged if you don't get the results you were looking for. It is possible that your expectations were unrealistic or you need to learn some more about audience targeting. If your ad reaches over 500 people daily, it will get a relevance score. Use the information on relevance scores to help improve your ads. Definitely experiment with A/B testing. Facebook calls this split testing and it is an available option when you set up your ad. Split testing consists of running two similar ads at the same time with subtle differences to see which option works the best. I use split testing to experiment with audiences.
- Know your own audience. Having a Facebook Page is necessary to get the benefit of data on your audience. Know them inside out. Find out how old are they, what gender, what countries do they live in. Analyze your posts to find out which are the most engaging (available in Facebook Insights). This helps you understand what your audience likes. Pay attention to what time of day they like and comment. Chances are other readers are there at the same time. Is there a day that is better than others? Remember, Facebook won't do this work for you, they just provide the data.
- Know the rules. Ads have specifics you are obligated to follow—character numbers in headlines, only 20% of your space can

be text, to name a couple. Pay attention to ads that catch your eye. What are they doing right?
- Learn how to track your results with the data that Facebook gives you. Learn how much you have to spend to reach your goals.
- Find a source for good images for your ads. You should probably pay for good ones. Try Shutterstock, iStockphotos, and others. Your cover artists might make a horizontal version of your cover for ads without charging you for a full cover again. Ask.
-

Types of Facebook ads that have worked well for my clients:

- Split test ads to build email lists (Minimum budget of $500 per campaign)
- Book sales ads that lead to Amazon page with targeted interest audience on the first weekend of launch (3 days at $50/day)
- Promoted posts. I know people don't think they should have to do it, but if you have thousands of followers, you should pay to boost a sales post that is getting good traction so more of your followers will see it and share. Always ask people to share—it's only a click. You will have to struggle with the 20% text rule here if you are using an image. I use these for sales and for awareness. Believe it or not, all your Facebook fans are not aware of everything going on because they don't all see your posts. I want to move them to the place where they do see my posts. Ads can help you get there over time.
- Book cover ads—if the covers are spectacular. I ask the cover artists to give me an image with no text except the title. This will help you get around the 20% text rule. Put the author name in the ad text. These are harder to put together visually because the ad holes are horizontal and book covers are usually vertical. It takes some practice.

Types of Facebook ads that have not worked for me:

- One-day promotions for book sales with a budget of less than $250.
- Email-gated one-day promotions. This means adding a newsletter sign-up as a contingency for getting a free book. This is a good strategy for the long run but not for a day.
- Ads whose audiences and budgets do not match. If you are trying to reach too many people with too little money, you are going to fail.
- Ads whose headlines do not have a call-to-action or benefit.
- Ads with pictures of people that are so small you cannot see their faces.

I know there are other ways to use Facebook ads, but I stick mostly to these. One thing I do know: if you want to spend only $10 a week to promote a book on Facebook, you probably won't succeed. That isn't even a good budget for reaching 100 percent of the people on your fan page.

Goodreads

I have yet to execute a successful ad with the new Self Serve Advertising option on Goodreads. But there are some reasons for that. First, my experience consists of two campaigns with one client. Both these campaigns were slated shortly after Goodreads opened up the platform, and it is still in its beginning stages. Second, there is only one option—cost per click—and your rate is set by Goodreads. One problem that I see is that people are not yet trained to buy books on Goodreads. It's like going to your book club with a sack of books to sell—it is just not native to the occasion, at least not yet. In both cases above, the ads never exhausted the budget that I set and there were no direct sales we could attribute. I convinced my client that we should wait and see if this platform gets any traction. At this time, I can't recommend Goodreads as an ad platform, but I am keeping an eye out for author success stories. Let me know if you have one.

Twitter

At this time, Twitter basically has three types of paid ads: promoted tweets, promoted accounts, and promoted trends. It's my feeling that none of these are smart options for authors. All three require enterprise-type budgets to make an impact at this point in time. If you want to try your hand with Twitter paid ads you will need to set up an account first, much like you would on Facebook.

There are better options for promoting books on Twitter and one is to incorporate free Twitter cards into your website or blog. These "cards" are tweets that are designed to draw attention by taking up more space on a Twitter feed with a summary of the link and an image or video. Marketers have been able to increase the engagement of a link significantly by using Twitter cards because the cards take up a larger space in a Twitter feed and are visual. All the cards require dropping a simple line of html code into the page that links to the tweet. It is a quick task that a web designer could do quickly. There are four types of Twitter cards that might interest authors. The definitions below were taken from Twitter's website:

- *Summary Cards*: "The Summary Card can be used for many kinds of web content, from blog posts and news articles, to products and restaurants. It is designed to give the reader a preview of your content before clicking through to your website." Below is an example of a summary card from my blog. To activate the Summary Card, your tweet must include a link. If the link includes an image, Twitter will also show the image. The only downside to these cards is that Twitter users can set the summaries to be hidden.

- *Summary Cards With Large Images*: "The Summary Card with Large Image features a large, full-width prominent image with a tweet. It is designed to give the reader a rich photo experience, and clicking on the image brings the user to the linked website." I actually like these better than the Summary Cards as this card features an image that stretches the width of the tweet and a click on the picture takes the viewer to the link. Be aware that if you have an image that does not fit the right dimensions (minimum of 280 by 150 pixels), the image will be cropped to that ratio and some of the image may be missing in the tweet. This image will not work well for a book cover unless the cover is part of a wider image that includes the cover. I recommend some experimenting if you want to go this route. Here is a sample of what it looks like:

- *Player Card:* "Video clips and audio streams have a special place on the Twitter platform thanks to the Player Card. By implementing a few HTML meta tags to your website and following the Twitter Rules of the Road, you can deliver your rich media to users across the globe." If you produce video, this might be a good option for you. Just be sure to read through the guidelines as Twitter will only approve your card based on those policies.

The nice thing about Twitter cards is that they are free. They will work for authors who have a website or blog that can accept code. Unfortunately, you cannot drop a piece of code into your book page on Amazon.

Pinterest

Pinterest just announced that a Buy Button is coming to their platform in the future. Right now, the feature is being tested with selected large brands. There will be an ad interface for people who want to use it as you will need to connect your products to their pay system somehow. I am interested to see if one of the big online retailers (Amazon, Kobo, iTunes) links with this system. There are not enough details yet to answer those questions. I think it will be a boon for authors who sell their own books already. But honestly, you can already sell books from Pinterest in just two clicks by sending readers directly to your book's buy page on Amazon from an image on your Pinterest board.

A Pinterest board can easily be set up to look like a bookstore with covers, short book descriptions, reviews, and a buy link with every pin. I know an author who claims Pinterest is a good source of direct book sales. She gets this feedback from some of her most invested fans. In addition to a catalog sales board, she pins her blog pieces, her book research, recipes, and much more. Also, she promotes her email newsletter signup there as well. She has identified Pinterest as a commerce channel, so it is maintained regularly, cross-promoted, and used for book launches. It does take maintenance and work, so be aware of the investment as you plan. Pinterest is an emerging channel for fiction authors and I expect to see more authors using the channel for direct sales in the future.

Cover Ads and Review Blogs

Many review blogs sell ads, and some of them have excellent reach and loyal followers. Make sure you know the reach numbers (monthly page views) and subscriber numbers. I've had some success with clients using cover ads on targeted review blogs for as little as $50 a month. You just have to do your research and know where your readers are. The trick here is measuring sales. I use them in the post-launch phase when sales have leveled off so I can monitor sales spikes. Some banner ads run for three days, some for a month, depending on the site and your budget. This is an "experiment and figure it out" option in my thinking.

Action Steps

1. If you have a blog and a Twitter account, consider implementing Twitter cards for your blog pieces. Do some research and see if you are able to add the necessary code yourself. If not, consider hiring a website person to help.
2. Have you used Facebook ads? Go back over one of your ad campaigns and make notes about what worked and what didn't. Consider taking a free course (like Mark Dawson's) on how to use Facebook ads to build your email list.
3. Do some research and find review blogs in your genre that have large followings and make note if they have any sponsorship abilities you can take advantage for a book launch.

Chapter 19: A Word Of Caution About Social Media Ads

Most of my ideas in this chapter first appeared as a guest blog on the Writer Beware site which is expertly curated by Victoria Strauss. Her blog is a source of reliable information on worthless schemes aimed at authors. She describes her blog as "Shining a bright light into the dark corners of the shadow-world of literary scams, schemes, and pitfalls. Also providing advice for writers, industry news and commentary, and a focus on the weird and wacky things that happen at the fringes of the publishing world." I get email from authors who are frustrated. They see social media as a minefield and don't want to step in for fear they will never come out. Sometimes the easiest thing to do is just buy that package of hundreds of tweets for twenty dollars and cross your fingers hoping that somebody will buy your book. After all, everybody says you have to be on Twitter, right? How can an author make sense of the noise on the internet and decide what, if anything, to do?   **Separate the Wheat From the Chaff** My husband is a grain farmer. Every year we pull out the massive combine and get it ready for the magic of harvest. Those mountainous machines cut the grain and feed it through a mechanism that separates the grain from its stalk while farmers ride in air conditioned comfort. The stalks are chewed up into chaff and spewed out the back of the combine to be absorbed back into the soil.

In marketing, we need to do the same. We have to learn how to separate the wheat from the chaff. We need to learn how to spot a worthless marketing scheme. But there's a learning curve. And sometimes that Facebook ad that worked for your friend isn't going to work for you. This is where education comes in. The book marketing sector, more than any I have ever worked in, is full of bad marketing advice. My objective here is to help you separate the wheat from the chaff—to be able to spot snake oil when you see it.
It's the Principle of the Thing   Every business sector has best practices. It's possible to circumvent those and get a

modicum of success, but why would you? Trust the best practices as a place to start. They aren't rocket science, they are just based on data. Take this example on hashtags. In early 2014, Dan Zarella, a social media researcher for HubSpot, found that if hashtags are used in a tweet (a pound sign followed by a tag with no spaces), that tweet is 55 percent more likely to be retweeted than one with no hashtags. His results were based on mining data from over one million tweets. So, people jumped on the hashtag bandwagon. The more, the better, or so people thought.

In 2014 Buffer, another reliable social media research company, published data indicating that after two hashtags, engagement of a post actually goes down (graphic below courtesy of Buffer).

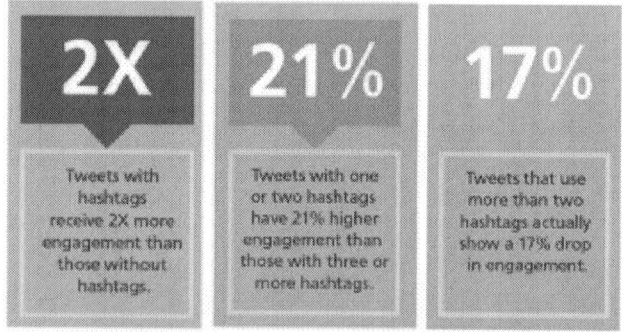

This is a principle that professional marketers take for granted now. But there are some uninformed marketing salespeople out there telling authors that the more hashtags the merrier.

An ad from a site called Unlimited Tweet Generator constantly retweeted by many authors reads:

Unlimited Tweet Generator mixes an unlimited number of brackets, producing as many hashtags as your can fit into your 140 character limit. Tweet example: Great book http://...#one #two #three #four #five #six #seven etc. That many hashtags will spread your message to many millions of people generating a truly astonishing amount of traffic.

And, for a mere 20 bucks or so, you can buy a day's worth of tweets loaded with hashtags from beginning to end that will do absolutely nothing but get ignored. All these hashtag-laden tweets do is annoy people. To the savvy social media user, they reek of stupidity. The outlier may sell a few books, but they probably can't be attributed to this scam.

Another popular Twitter scam offered by more than one company offers authors hundreds of thousands of followers worth of exposure for your tweet for a fee. I experimented with one of these snake oil outfits recently just to test it. I knew I was blowing my money, but it was a mere twenty bucks to prove my thesis. Their packages are seen below:

Bronze	Silver	Gold	Platinum	Diamond
$19	$36	$51	$64	$75
1 DAY OF TWEETS	2 DAYS OF TWEETS	3 DAYS OF TWEETS	4 DAYS OF TWEETS	5 DAYS OF TWEETS
✓ 1 DAY	✓ 2 DAYS	✓ 3 DAYS	✓ 4 DAYS	✓ 5 DAYS
✓ 36 TWEETS	✓ 72 TWEETS	✓ 108 TWEETS	✓ 144 TWEETS	✓ 180 TWEETS
✓ 375,000+ FOLLOWERS	✓ 375,000+ FOLLOWERS	✓ 375,000+ FOLLOWERS	✓ 375,000+ FOLLOWERS	✓ 375,000+ FOLLOWERS
✓ BOOK EXPOSURE	✓ MORE EXPOSURE	✓ GREAT EXPOSURE	✓ GREATER EXPOSURE	✓ HUGE EXPOSURE!
Get Started!	Get Started!	Get Started!	Get Started!	Get Started!

This company boasts three different Twitter accounts with 375,000 followers. I want to add that it is fairly easy to amass Twitter followers if you know what you are doing. For instance, this particular company is supposedly followed by LeBron James, according to the report I ran on their followers on the Simply Measured website. But the real LeBron James only follows 184 people. So, on a whim I looked through them all. This company was not listed in people Mr. James follows. This LeBron James page is a fake auto-follow account built to help people pad their follower numbers by automatically following back everyone that follows them. Twitter is littered with these fake accounts that automatically follow back so other unscrupulous people can amass large follower counts. It's a well-known racket called *follower farms*. Fake follower companies search diligently for these auto-following accounts to increase their fake reach. (Did you notice I use the word fake a lot?) Unethical companies can then use their fake padded numbers to put together silly promotions like this one. Also, an analysis of this company's top 20 influencers did not produce one account that would be in the market for my books. My $19 produced zero sales and zero new Twitter followers. Maybe I should have spent more money. But alas, here's a review from an author that purchased a five-day tweet package: http://godchild.buzz/booktweeters/. Also no sales. Scam artists know what they are doing. They are playing on people's pain points and ignorance. They can build fake followings completely on accounts that follow back automatically. Keep in mind that all you need to start a Twitter account is an email address. It's an ugly, dark business. There is no verification to make sure that real people are setting up accounts. These companies abound on the internet. Hint: if their website looks like it was put up in ten minutes and has no names of real people behind the company or an about page with contact information, beware.

We Will Promote Your Book… For a Price

There are more bad promotion sites out there than you can shake a stick at, as my Grandma used to say. How can you tell the difference between the good, the bad, and the ugly? Many of them have slick websites, Facebook pages, and multiple Twitter feeds boasting thousands, maybe millions of followers. Here are a couple pointers to help you make up your mind.

1. Good sites: There are many sites out there that are based on good marketing principles and have a large audience of both authors and readers. They validate their expertise with blog pieces, authentic peer recommendations, podcasts, books they write, webinars, speaking engagements, and they prove success by numbers over a long period of time. The resource may be membership-gated, such as Jim Kukral's Author Marketing Club (I am a member), Where

Writers Win, and others. They usually offer a subscription at a reasonable yearly price and offer a large variety of tools to help authors succeed. There are also many knowledgeable marketing consultants who cater strictly to authors. You can probably get recommendations from author friends, people you meet at workshops, and on author forums. Consultants will do anything from write your book descriptions to set up social media profiles and manage your social media campaigns. I recommend doing your homework before hiring a consultant, but I do recommend you set aside a budget and outsource tasks that you don't have time or expertise to do. Consultants often validate their expertise through publishing a blog, writing books, hosting podcasts, writing guest blogs, and posting customer testimonials. I can write my own book descriptions but I pay a copywriter a reasonable fee so I can save myself the time and get an expert result it would take me much longer to craft. Also in the good category are many author forums like Writer's Cafe (KBoards) and The Alliance of Independent Authors (I am a member). Forums like these are a good place to get recommendations and reviews for everything from editors to marketing services. Also, many author organizations have private moderated forums that can be a good source of information.

The most reliable source of information on scams aimed at authors is the *Writer Beware* website curated by Victoria Strauss at http://accrispin.blogspot.com/.

2. Questionable sites (the bad and the ugly): It is impossible to list all the suspect author marketing services out there. Many of these sites ask for money for their suspect services. There is no information on their "about" pages that validates their expertise or existence, just blabbing about the reach of their audience. They are not published authors or even legitimate marketing services. They operate product-only websites that talk about "we", but you can't find a real name anywhere on the site. Beware of offers like this one from ContentMo.com: http://bit.ly/1FZbTPg. Besides the fact that their website design is a red flag, their claim that they have 23 million impressions a month on social media is irrelevant. There is no explanation or proof of who or where those impressions come from other than a list of their interconnected Twitter feeds and low-volume Facebook pages. Another common red flag here is the absence of real people's names in the About section of their site, a Gmail address as a contact, no address or location information, and their testimonials are suspect. I am also wondering why a company that brags 23 million impressions a month has only 167 likes on their Facebook page. Many sites in this category have some free services. If you want to give them a try, keep track of your results. I do recommend recording results with every marketing strategy you try. If they are free, give them more than one try so you can make sure your initials results were correct. Free is okay, but you often get what you pay for…nothing.

Action Steps

1. Find the Writer Beware website (http://accrispin.blogspot.com/) and subscribe to updates. There is a sign-up box in the right tab on the blog. This is the best way to keep up on all the latest scams aimed at writers.
2. If you ever find a social media scam online, send me an email (chris@cksyme.com). I am always interested in researching and writing blog pieces about unethical services aimed at authors.

Chapter 20: SMART Resources: People And Companies That You Can Trust

Part of learning how to be successful at marketing your books is developing a lifelong learning habit. Things change, people find better ways to communicate, audience behaviors change, technologies evolve. In order to keep up, develop the habit of learning.

I've put together a list of resources to help authors be solid advice on marketing strategies. I have tried to limit the list to just the best resources I believe deliver useful marketing advice applicable to authors. I am housing that list on my website here: http://bit.ly/1Low4bk . Choose a few that make the most sense to you. A good resource arsenal should include the following:

Blogs

I follow a lot of blogs. I have a slight case of FOMO. Because I like to share helpful links with my followers on Twitter, I spend a chunk of time every morning reading marketing articles. I have found the best way to do this is by using an RSS reader. RSS stands for *real simple syndication* and it is a process that delivers a blog's feed directly to a list you can skim and by category. I do subscribe to some blogs via email as well but this is the most manageable way to stay in touch with your favorite blogs. Even if you are not a professional marketer, an RSS reader is a huge time saver.

There are a number of RSS reader apps out there that will deliver and organize blogs you want to follow. All you have to do is input the blog's home page URL in the reader and it will pull the newly published articles into your reader whenever they are published. I use and recommend Feedly (www.feedly.com). It has an easy user interface and a good organizational dashboard. I skim read the intro and headlines to decide if the full article is worth my time. If I think the article might be helpful to my followers, I read the full article and schedule a tweet to promote it. If I want to save it for reference, I link it to my Readability account that lets me read it later or send it to my Kindle.

Most people start out following too many blogs and don't have time to read everything. The truth is if you follow just a few good ones, you'll get the same information as you would following many. In the resource list on my website, I asterisk the resources I believe are essential. I have resources aimed at authors only and general marketing resources that authors can benefit from.

Podcasts

I listen to a number of good podcasts but only a few regularly. I honestly don't have time to listen to all that I would like. I scan show notes first to see if the material looks relevant. If it isn't, I don't listen. I just don't have 45 extra minutes to listen to something I'm not sure will be helpful. The podcasts I recommend on my resource list are strictly aimed at authors.

Books

I also included a selected list of books. The books on this list are only must-read books—ones that will not waste your time. Some of these books are aimed at authors and some of them are general social media marketing books. Some of the best resources for authors are not aimed at authors.

The List Is Not Exclusive

Because this list is a work in progress, I am always looking for recommendations for good resources. I don't claim that it is exhaustive by any means. You can leave a note for me in the Facebook group I've set up if you have a good resource you'd like to share. You will find out how to join at the end of the book. Bottom line: never stop learning. The link to the resources page is here: http://bit.ly/1Low4bk

Action Steps

1. Find the Social Media Examiner website (http://www.socialmediaexaminer.com/) and subscribe to updates. The sign-up is a menu item on the top header of their website labeled "free updates." This website is by far the best out there for all around social media advice.
2. Subscribe to my blog updates at cksyme.com. The email sign-up is on the right tab on my website and labeled, "get blog updates via email". I publish one or two time per week in addition to my weekly tip sheets which comes out over the weekend.

Bonus Material

1. **SMART Social Media Marketing Facebook Group:** This is a special Facebook group set up exclusively for you where authors can share their social media questions and their success stories. It is a private moderated group. Just search SMART Social Media For Authors on Facebook and you'll be there.

2. SMART Marketing Resources For Authors: A page of links to blogs, podcasts, and other resources just for authors. Copy this link into a browser: http://cksyme.com/smart-social-media-marketing-resources/.

Finally, I encourage you to follow me on social media. I am on Twitter **@cksyme** and my Pinterest channel is **CKSyme Media Group**. I write regularly on my blog at **cksyme.com** and would love to connect with you on any of those channels.

Action Steps

1. Join the SMART Social Media For Authors Facebook Group: https://www.facebook.com/groups/499804016845739/
2. Send me an email at chris@cksyme.com letting me know what your biggest marketing challenge is and I will use your input to write upcoming blogs and weekly tip sheets. Don't be shy. I want to know exactly what you need to be successful.
3. If you liked the book, I would like to invite you to write a review on Amazon, Goodreads, or other bookstore of your choice. If you didn't like the book, please email me at chris@cksyme.com and let me know your thoughts. I appreciate all input.

Thanks for buying the book. Now the real work starts. Take what you have learned and put it into practice. If you didn't sign up for the Bonus Content, go back and do that now. It will be a real motivator for your success as a SMART social media marketer. Please keep in touch. I want to hear your successes as well as your frustrations. You know where to find me.

A Word Of Thanks…

Nobody knows better than authors that when you write a book it is not a solo project. I want to thank my author-daughter who writes historical romance under the name R.L. Syme and romantic suspense under the name Becca Boyd for her part in this project. To me she is Becca, and she has helped me navigate the world of indie authors.

Thanks to Cherilyn and *Got Your Back Editing* for the watchful eye and attention to detail and the Killon Group for the great cover. Also thanks to Bryan Cohen for my masterful book description. Many thanks go to my husband who patiently endured many meals of cereal (which he secretly loves anyway) while I shut myself in my office for hours on end. And thanks mostly to those of you that bought this book. You are the true champion entrepreneurs and the reason I do what I do. May this book bring you increased success in everything you do related to writing.

-Chris Syme

Copyright © 2015 Chris Syme

All rights reserved under International and Pan-American Copyright Conventions

This is a work of fiction. All characters and events portrayed in this book are fictional and a product of the author's imagination. Any similarities to real people, living or dead, is purely coincidental and unintentional.

By payment of required fees, you have been granted the *non-*exclusive, *non-*transferable right to access and read the text of this book. No part of this text may be reproduced, transmitted, downloaded, decompiled, reverse engineered, or stored in or introduced into any information storage and retrieval system, in any form or by any means, whether electronic or mechanical, now known or hereinafter invented without the express written permission of copyright owner.

Please Note

The reverse engineering, uploading, and/or distributing of this book via the internet or via any other means without the permission of the copyright owner is illegal and punishable by law. Please purchase only authorized electronic editions, and do not participate in or encourage electronic piracy of copyrighted materials. Your support of the author's rights is appreciated.

No part of this book may be reproduced or transmitted in any form or by any electronic or mechanical means, including photocopying, recording or by any information storage and retrieval system, without the written permission of the publisher, except where permitted by law.

Interior format by The Killion Group
http://thekilliongroupinc.com

Made in the USA
Middletown, DE
13 February 2018